saltcity
Cádiz Field+Work 2006-2008

Suzanne Ewing
Architecture, University of Edinburgh, Edinburgh, UK

contents

saltcity Field+Work 2006-2008

3. Stone detail, Royal Saltworks at Arc-et-Senans, France (Claude-Nicholas Ledoux 1775-79). Image: copyright.

foreword

The University of Edinburgh has offered professional training in architecture since the mid-1960s when architect Sir Robert Matthew established the Architecture school. Since that time, the school has grown in size and diversity. It now offers a range of undergraduate degrees in architecture, architectural history and structural engineering with architecture. In addition, it supports a large PhD programme (by text and/or design) and a range of MSc programmes in areas such as architectural and urban design, digital media, sound design, sustainable design, and project management. The school also actively collaborates with a number of other subject areas in the University such as art history, music, film studies and engineering. These collaborations will be enriched further from next year under an "Academic Federation" between the University of Edinburgh and the Edinburgh College of Arts (eca). From that time, the school will combine with neighbouring architecture and landscape architecture programmes at eca, and with built environment programmes at Heriot-Watt University to offer a setting for architectural education that spans the creative arts and built environment sciences. It is an exciting initiative that will deepen and diversify the opportunities for architectural study in Scotland.

The school at Edinburgh has developed a unique character that combines cosmopolitanism, situated practices, research-led approaches to teaching and learning, and a spirit of intellectual risk-taking and creative inquiry. This character emerges from a number of factors: the school's location in an ancient, research-intensive university, the creativity and skill of its academic staff, the excellent students it attracts, and its setting in the remarkable city of Edinburgh itself. This character comes into sharp focus in the MArch programme and finds particular expression in the work that you will see in the following pages.

Stephen Cairns, Head of Architecture, University of Edinburgh

The University of Edinburgh's Master of Architecture programme as it exists today is the result of a twenty-year process of pedagogical transformation and refinement. The final-year studio's focus on the city was first definitively established in the late 1980s, and the implications of this were worked through for a sequence of cities over the next ten years. In 2000 the idea of an overarching programmatic theme that would co-ordinate the work was introduced, first for a studio based around Ghent (*Architecture as a Spatial Operator*) and then post-9/11 Berlin (*Architecture in the Age of Anxieties*). By this stage the programme, and indeed the department more generally, was attracting significant international attention for its approach - see, for example, the review published in the Japanese journal *Architecture + Urbanism*, 413 (2000).

A few years later certain structural changes that were taking place in the university allowed the opportunity to reconfigure the MArch into its present distinctive two-year format. The first of the new studios was based around Valletta (2004-2006) and led by Adrian Hawker; the second around Shanghai (2005-2007) and led by Dorian Wiszniewski. The Cádiz studio - the subject of this volume - is then the third of the series. The present catalogue, which inaugurates a new sequence of yearly publications based on the MArch programme, richly documents both the students' work and the reflective and critical pedagogy of the studio leader, Suzanne Ewing, assisted by Victoria Clare Bernie who has been a consistent and key member of the MArch staff throughout its various transformations.

What seems to me crucial to the MArch programme at Edinburgh is the kind of "structured openness" that it offers its students, providing them with a powerful framework of enquiry without presupposing specific answers. From the outset this permits the city itself to be posed as a question and the studio - thrillingly - to run as a collective endeavour of exploration and research in which students and tutors are active participants, while the two-year timing allows the projects to emerge in dialogue with a programme of cultural, historical, and material research of startling depth and intensity.

Mark Dorrian, MArch Programme Director, University of Edinburgh

introduction: field

saltcity Field+Work 2006-2008

This catalogue documents the first exhibition of design work from the Master of Architecture (MArch) Programme at the University of Edinburgh that has been curated explicitly for a wider viewing public. It is a record of original research practice that seeks to provide an insight into the pedagogy and processes distinctive to the *Cádiz Field+Work* design studio 2006-2008. The structure of the MArch Programme at the University of Edinburgh seeks to integrate research and design in the production of an architectural proposal for a specified European city. It actively encourages engagement with: medium, history, culture, geography, narrative, politics, technology and art. The Architecture that is produced in the programme is described in various media: drawings, paintings, photographs, sketches, models, films, animations, descriptive and analytical texts, theoretical essays, installations and performances. It describes an intellectual and imaginative territory at once familiar and unsettling to a discipline whose more recent traditions have borrowed from, rather than inhabited, the visual devices and theoretical investigations of other disciplines.

SaltCity: Cádiz Field+Work is structured around a two-year chronology of the studio, drawing attention to key aspects of the thematic structure and highlighting significant pieces of design and research. The narrative begins with **+Work (landschaft)**, an opening up of the notion of the eidetic in relation to design projects, fieldwork and research. **Hinge 1** depicts a key collective project that calls into question issues of temporality and multiplicity in relation to the urban. **+Work (mēchanē)** reflects on relationships between analysis, interpretation and irrigation as the group city strategies migrate towards individual spatial strategies, scaled environmental and technological testing. **Hinge 2** consolidates propositions in a 1:500 City Model as a generative locus for the final integrative design, exhibition and report, the subject of the closing discussion in **+Work (praxis)**. Eight individual project enquiries have been selected for exhibition, serving to elucidate aspects of the studio narrative. The main text by the programme leader is interwoven with other voices - student reflections, commentators on Cádiz, studio contributors and provocative extracts from recent architectural discourse.

"I visited the *SaltCity* studio on two occasions during the programme. I saw many inventive schemes and ambitious ideas, and the variety impressed me. But what I enjoyed more, and what stayed with me afterwards, was the deeper contribution that this pedagogy makes to studio teaching, and to architecture in the broadest sense. *SaltCity* demonstrates a learning modality that - for all its forward-looking vision - takes us back to an architectural culture steeped in humanist traditions.

What impressed me about the studio was a credo of social ethics that permeated everything. I found this ethical approach all the more interesting because it was entirely buried in a mode of design practice. Thus, projects were not trying to 'do good' or earn brownie points. Rather, their engagement with reality wanted to make a better world.

The idea of making a better world, rather than other mainstream models of success - such as being a solid professional; providing good value for the client; commercial reliability and effectiveness - is a rare thing in architectural practice, but it is a powerful paradigm for the orientation of architecture as a discipline. This programme has been especially successful in bringing ethical approaches to bear on typical yet contemporary urban problems, especially problems of civic order that account for the interface between sustainability concerns and society's need for cultural continuity. By drawing out local stories and the character of particular situations, the studiowork embeds its proposals in a grounded reality. This truth to experience then typically injects a sense of place into efforts to envisage a positive future. Designs for something new are anchored not only in context, but also in care. And this care - a duty to make the world a better place - becomes a 'duty of care' exercised in the work of imagining.

There is no greater and more endemic failure in contemporary urban development than the failure of imagination. *SaltCity* demonstrates a studio methodology in which invention and subtlety are not simply flourishes in an otherwise empty vocabulary of talent, but a fusion of aesthetics and ethics. This is the value of treating the studio as a venue for investigating where theory and practice come together; somewhere between field research and exercises in conceptualisation. The achievement of *SaltCity* is to anchor even the most frivolous of its vignettes in a consolidated structure of understanding, one that reinserts the human story into its dream for reinvigorating a city that has lost its bloom."

Matthew Barac, Architect, PTEa (London), Chairman, Architecture sans Frontières (UK)

frame of a shopping trolley)
12:56- Rain stops. 4 Umbrellas in bin, 2 on floor, 2 being held. c. 20 sold. Large pile of wrappers
12:57- Men/umbrellas/bin/wrappers gone

6. Immigrant umbrella sellers. Image: Mike Whitfield. 7. Men on bench. Image: Craig Hutchinson

field. n. the territory belonging to a city[1]

The Master of Architecture Programme at the University of Edinburgh plays out over two academic years of four semesters and one summer. The structure and content of the programme defines the Architectural Design Studio as a ground for exploration and experimentation within the potentially more didactic confines of the wider educational and professional context.[2] It takes as its point of departure the study city, the empirical anchor, a site chosen for its potential as a rich territory: an architecture, a city, a climate, a politics, a history, an industry, a language and a culture capable of informing an understanding of a contemporary urban (European) condition. A field trip took place in November of the first semester. The *Hinge* projects - collective endeavours across the studio - took place in January of Semesters 2 and 4. The work of the studio is a shifting ground of workshop, design studio, computing lab, library, archive and field. Students work independently and collectively in directed and self-directed contexts.

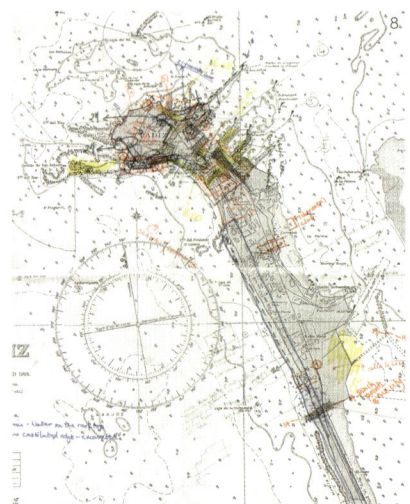

Studio practice was guided by the notions of engagement, negotiation and narrative set down by the French social scientist and philosopher Michel de Certeau in *The Practice of Everyday Life*.[3] Here strategic, tactical (and in-between) ways of operating as an individual in a city are seen to represent a potential for the critical architectural project; to evoke the possibility of a generative understanding between urban research (analysis) and architectural design (projection/speculation/inhabitation). The teaching philosophy in the *Cádiz Field+Work* programme is underpinned by a commitment to collaboration, dialogue, and Architecture as *praxis*.[4]

The 2006-2008 studio theme of *Cádiz Field+Work* is premised on a need and desire for architectural design practice to be self-consciously situated. Rem Koolhaas talks of the future role of architecture as "the irrigation of territories with potential" rather than "the arrangement of more or less permanent objects".[5] This statement provokes an exploratory approach to understanding: territory (field, ground, site); what "potential" might be (programmatic attitude); what might constitute acts of "irrigation" (erasure, purging, resistance, friction, intervention, augmentation, accretion). The challenge of the work is primarily one of engagement, of the critical activation of the imaginative potential of the city as: an idea, a cultural history, a particular topography and an array of technological possibilities.

The University of Edinburgh Masters of Architecture Programme 2006-2008 has collaborated with the Colegio de Arquitectos de Cádiz and leading academics and practitioners from Scotland, England, America and Spain.

1 Oxford English Dictionary (Oxford University Press, Oxford, 2008)
2 Ewing, S "Between the strategic and the tactical: research driven projects and project driven researches in Cádiz/Edinburgh" paper presented at EAAE International Conference *The Urban Project* (TU Delft, 4-7 June 2008)
3 de Certeau, M *The Practice of Everyday Life* trans. Rendall, S (University of California Press, Berkeley, 1984)
4 Pérez-Gómez, A "Architecture and Ethics Beyond Globalization" ARCC/EAAE Montreal Conference on Architectural Research eds Fontein, L, Neukerman, H (Belgium, 2001) pp13-22
5 Koolhaas, R, OMA "Whatever Happened to Urbanism?" *SMLXL* (010 Publishers, Rotterdam, 1995)

8. Field work: identifying territories of concern. Image: Suzanne Ewing. 9. Metropolitan Bay network (Adam Collier). 10. Cádiz as global punta (Mike Whitfield)

Cádiz is an Atlantic city on the southwestern coast of Europe. The Bahia de Cádiz - comprising the city on the isthmus and four other towns - is currently perceived as one metropolitan area. It is a condition which raises questions of the definition of urban field within a loose city:land:aqueous topography. Historically Cádiz was a centre of the Phoenician salt trade, a Roman city and a key gateway for the Americas. Until 1884 it was a prime nautical meridian: a significant cosmopolitan pivot in the cultures of discovery and globalisation; a *punta* or point of Europe, Africa and the Americas; a testing ground of military and naval tactics and a portal for flows of goods, people and ideas. It is a city of the south, a peninsula of the peninsula of Spain. It is *not* an island, it is a landform set apart from yet tethered to mainland Spain, a territory historically perceived of as "other" to Europe. Its Atlantic situation conditions it as a place of raw exposure - salt, wind and light - and fragile ecologies - fish, wetland and coastal shelf. The city of Cádiz is the decadent scion to an extreme environment. What does it mean to cultivate dwelling and public life in this context? How might this cosmopolitan ground be "irrigated with potential" through thoughtful, maybe radical, architectural and urban engagement?

The high-speed AVE train currently connects the 550km from Madrid to Sevilla in 2.5 hours. From Sevilla to Cádiz a car, train or bus journey connection is 1.5 to 2 hours. Crossings from southern Mediterranean Spain to Africa take under 1 hour. The studio travelled from Edinburgh to Malaga (2148km) by plane in 3.5 hours, then to Cádiz (147 miles) by bus in 2.5 hours. It is a metropolitan area relatively disconnected by land yet strategically connected by sea. In a likely future where current decadent mobilities - particularly cheap air travel and centralised land-based infrastructure - cannot be taken for granted, can *SaltCity*, where *sal*(t) relates to salary, material production to time and land limits, offer clues and uncover potential for the generation of more meaningful relations between everyday life, production and spatiality? As salt is an agent of slowing (or speeding) decay, adding wit, drawing out existing taste, how might architecture be an agent of tactical resistance in slowing the city, adding surprise and delight, poetically drawing out existing attributes and posing new possibilities for dwelling and public life?

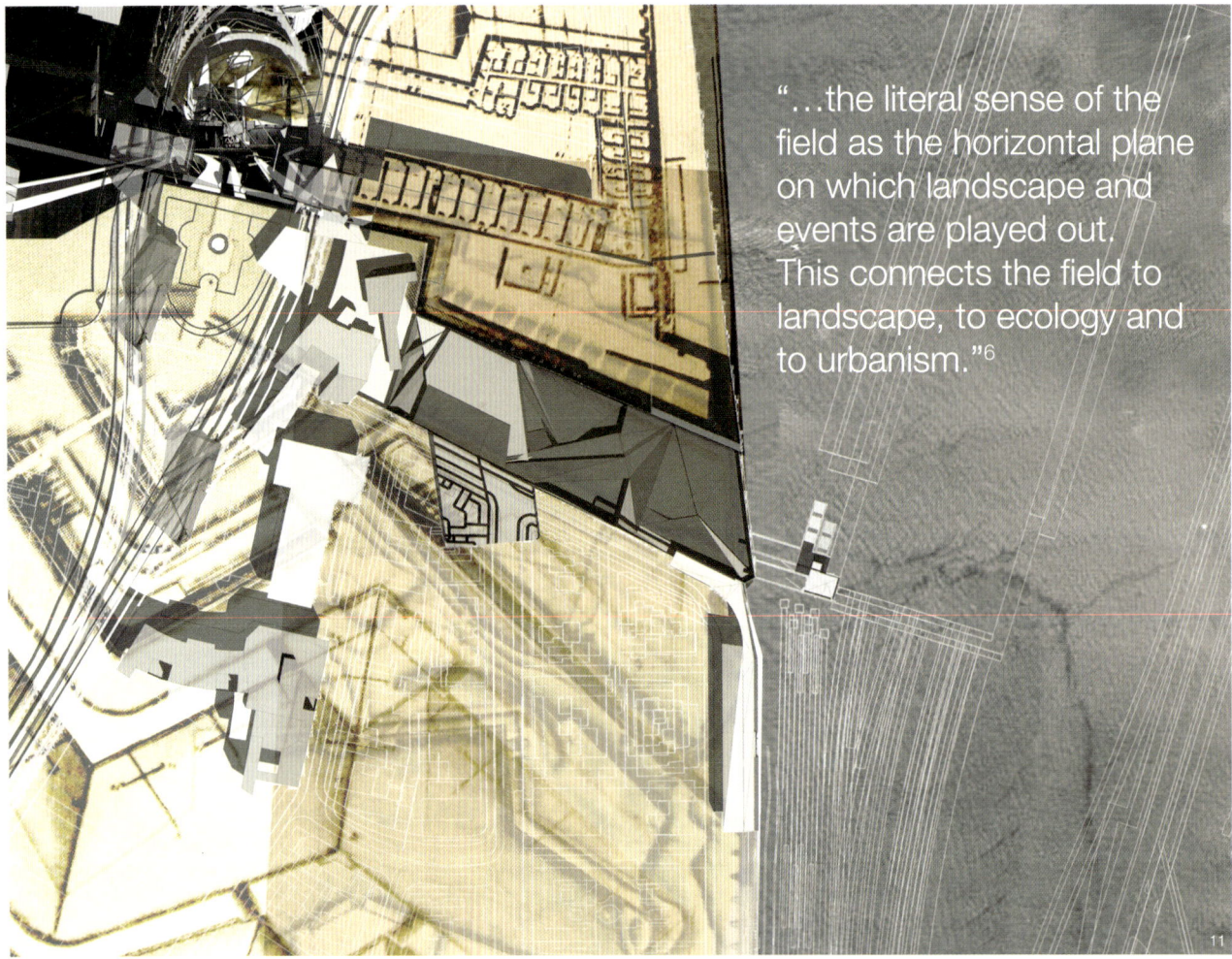

"…the literal sense of the field as the horizontal plane on which landscape and events are played out. This connects the field to landscape, to ecology and to urbanism."[6]

6   Allen, S "field conditions" *Assemblage* Issue 41 p8

"A cantilevering island, heavy mass floating, in tension."

Emma Bush, Sofi Tegsveden, Ross Perkin

11. Reprogramming the Ruptured City, plan a: Puerta de Tierra (Adam Collier). 12. Calle San Francisco. Image: Victoria Clare Bernie

"The nauseous effluvia of oil and garlick…I had suddenly been dropped from the clouds into the mist of a large masquerade…The floors are paved with brick, the rooms dark, and consequently cool, with large windows opening into balconies towards the street…The best houses have brick floors and stone or marble stairs. As the windows generally look into the patio or court, they are private and retired; and under the house is a cistern which, in the rainy season, is filled with water. Every dwelling is a separate castle, and capable of military defence. The streets of this city are remarkably well paved, which may in some measure arise from there being few or no wheel carriages to destroy the pavement…As this city is on a peninsular, at the termination of a long sandy isthmus, there is no ground unoccupied, and little can be spared for squares."[7]

13

14

15

12

13. Ostionera stone. Image: Suzanne Ewing. 14. Casa Patio Research. Image: Ross Perkin
15. Market. Image: Victoria Clare Bernie. 16. Port of Cádiz field studies (Annabel Cremer)

"You are already at sea, in Cádiz. You lean your elbows on the rail of a white city afloat in the blue, launched well out into the space from the land."[8]

"'This arch', she continued, 'is all that remains of the old castle. It was constructed on the site of an ancient Roman ampitheater, and it houses the Company of Guardimarinas. The professors and men in charge of the observatory were famous sailors and men of science. Jorge Juan and Antonio de Ulloa had published their work on the measurement of a degree of the meridian of the Equator, Mazarredo was a excellent naval tactitian, Malaspina was about to undertake his famous voyage, Tofiño was preparing the definitive hydrographic atlas of the Spanish coastline...' She turned in a circle, taking in her surroundings, and her voice was sad. 'It all ended at Trafalgar.'

They walked a little further into the alley. White bedding hung overhead between balconies, like motionless winding sheets in the night."[9]

7   William Jacob, on arriving in Cádiz, *Travels in the south of Spain*
    (London, 1811) Letter II pp9-10
8   Samuel Eliot Morrison, *Christopher Columbus, Mariner* (London, Faber
    & Faber, 1956) p110
9   Pérez-Reverte, A *The Nautical Chart* (Picador, 2002) p175

Cádiz Archive

Bibliography Compiled by MArch students, January 2007

Historical References

While not comprehensive, much historical information can be gleaned from old geographical and topographical accounts of Spain. The Edinburgh University Library has a selection shelved under 0.91(46) onwards incl:

Blazquez, A & Delagado-Aquilera *Peninsula Iberica* (La Real Sociedad Geografica 2nd ed, Barcelona) pp561-3
[Information on local industries and populations of towns of the whole of the Bay]

Dumas, A *From Paris to Cádiz* trans. March, A. E (Peter Owen Ltd, London 1856/1958) pp207-213

Finck, HT *Spain and Morocco* pp58-74 (Percival & Co, London 1891)
[Late 19th Century account of Cádiz and local industries, incl. sherry manufacture pp64-5 and salt pans pp66-67]

Hutton, E *The Cities of Spain* (Methuen and Co, London c.1930)
[Esp. Chapter XIX pp250-252 Impressionistic description of early 20th century Cádiz]

Sykes, WH "Statistics of Cádiz" *Journal of the Statistical Society of London* Volume 1 October 1838

History of Spain

Shelfmark DP94 onwards in the Edinburgh University Library has a wide selection of books tracing the history of Spain from pre-history through to modern day cultural studies. These include more general works.

Blinkhorn, M *Democracy and Civil War in Spain 1931-1939* (Routledge, London 1992)
[Brief, but comprehensive, account of the Spanish War]

Elliott, JH *The Old World and the New 1492-1650* (Cambridge University Press, London 1970)

Farouk OF (ed.) *Aspects from Abbasid History* (2003)

Gilmour, D *The Transformation of Spain: From Franco to the Constitutional Monarchy* (Quartet Books, London 1985)

Graham, H *The Spanish Civil War: A Very Short Introduction* (Oxford University Press, Oxford 2005)

Preston, P *The Spanish Civil War 1936-1939* (Weidenfeld and Nicolson, London 1990)

Perez-Reverte, A *The Nautical Chart* (Picador, London 2002)

Tremlett, G *Ghosts of Spain* (Faber & Faber Ltd, London 2006)

History of Cádiz

Jauregui, JP "Cádiz, Punta de Europa" *Outline history of Cádiz* (Rosalibros, Seville 1999) pp21-59
[Historical and Architectural guide to Cádiz, in Spanish]

Paul EJ Hammer "Myth-Making: Politics, Propaganda and the Capture of Cádiz in 1596" *The Historical Journal* Vol 40 No.3, September 1997

Quijano, Cano, Viejo, Hernandez Palermo, *Cartografia de Cádiz* (Escuela de Estudios, Hispano-Americanos de Sevilla, Seville 1978)

Architecture of Spain

Bertolucci, C "Flamenco flair: Herzog & De Meuron" *Architectural Review* June 2004, *A+V* monographs Issue 114 VII-VIII 2005

Cabrero, GR *The Modern in Spain: Architecture after 1948* (The MIT Press, Cambridge MA 2001)

Dodds, JD *Architecture and Ideology in Early Medieval Spain* (The Pennsylvania State University Press, Pennsylvania 1990)

Hillenbrand, R *Islamic Architecture: form, function and meaning* (Edinburgh University Press, Edinburgh 2000,1994)

Kofman, E & Lebas, E (eds.) *Henri Lefebrve: Writings on Cities* "Rhythmanalysis of Mediterranean Cities" pp228-240 (Blackwells, Oxford 1996)

Lapunzina, A *Architecture of Spain* (Greenwood Press, 2005)

Mortada, H *Traditional Islamic Principles of Built Environment* (Routledge Curzon, 2003)

MVRDV *Costa Iberica: Upbeat to the Leisure City* (Actar, Barcelona 2002)

Riley, T (ed.) *On Site: New Architecture in Spain* (MOMA, New York, 2006)

General Information on Cádiz

Barragan, JM et al *Agua, Ciudad y Territorio* (Universidad de Cádiz, 1993) [Up to date and comprehensive geographical, oceanographic and geological information, in Spanish]

Mata, JJ & de Molina, JM *Guia Architectura de Cádiz* (Colegio Oficial de Architectos de Andalucia, Cádiz 1995)

Cultural Studies

Acton, T & Mundy, G *Romani Culture and Gypsy Identity* (University of Hertfordshire Press, Hatfield 1997)

Campion, JS *On Foot in Spain* (Chapman and Hall, London 1879) [Esp. Chapter XXXIII pp289-301 Detailed description of a rural carnival. Other chapters discuss differing aspects of late 19th Century Spanish rural life]

Corkhill, D. "Race, Immigration and Multiculturalism in Spain" in Jordan, B Morgan-Tamosunas, R (eds.) *Contemporary Spanish Cultural Studies* (Arnold, London 2000) pp48-57

Gilmore, D *Carnival and Culture: sex, symbol and status in Spain* (Yale University Press, London & New Haven 1998) [In-depth account of the Andalusian Carnaval, especially that of the ilegales. Concentrates on sexual and gender politics]

Hemingway, E *Death in the Afternoon* (Scribner, London 1932) [The most idiosyncratic Spanish spectacle as explained by an American, but by no means an outsider]

Kenrick, D *Gypsies: from the Ganges to the Thames* (University of Hertfordshire Press, Hatfield 2004)

Mintz, JR *Carnival Song and Society; Gossip, Sexuality and Creativity in Andalusia* (BERG Press, Washington 1997) [Account of the Carnival, especially the social aspects]

Moorhead, C *Human Cargo: A Journey Among Refugees* (Chatto & Windus, London, 2005)

Moreiras Menor, C "Spectacle, Trauma and Violence in Contemporary Spain" in Jordan, B Morgan-Tamosunas, R (eds.) *Contemporary Spanish Cultural Studies* (Arnold, London 2000) [A framework for artistic criticism for post-Franco Spanish culture]

Morgan, T "Memories and Modernities" in Jordan, B Morgan-Tamosunas, R (eds.) *Contemporary Spanish Cultural Studies* (Arnold, London 2000)

Pamuk, O *My Name is Red* (Faber & Faber, London 2001)

Okely, J *The Traveller-Gypsies* (Cambridge University Press, London, 1983)

Richards, M "Collective Memory, the nation-state and post-Franco Society" in Jordan, B Morgan-Tamosunas, R (eds.) *Contemporary Spanish Cultural Studies* (Arnold, London 2000)

Washabaugh, W *Flamenco, Passion, Politics and Popular Culture* (BERG Press, 1996)

Geography/Ecology/Geology

Benavente, J et al, "Coastal Flooding Hazard Related to Storms and Coastal Evolution in Valdelagrana Spit (Cádiz Bay Natural Park)" *Continental Shelf Research* 26, 2006, pp1061-1076

Butzer, KW "Irrigation Agrosystems in Eastern Spain: Roman or Islamic Origins?" *Annals of the association of American Geographers* Vol 75 no.4 Dec. 1985

Carrido Perez, MC et al, "Evaluating Seawater Quality Objectives: Application to the Andalucia Littoral", Bol. *Instituto Espanol de Oceanografia* pp523-530

Chica-Olmo, M et al, "Integrated Remote Sensing and GIS Techniques for biogeochemical characterization of the Tinto-Odiel Estuary System", *Environmental Geology* 45, 2004 pp834-842

Churchill, E "Semple, Irrigation and Reclamation in the Ancient Mediterranean Region", *Annals of the Association of American Geographers* Vol 75, no.4 Dec. 1985

David, RA et al, "Rio Tinto Estuary (Spain): 5000 Years of Pollution" *Environmental Geology* 39(10), Sept 2000 pp1107-1116

van Geen, A et al, "A 120 Year Record of Widespread Contamination from Mining of the Iberian Pyrite Belt", *Geology*, Vol 25 no.4 April 1997 pp291-294

Houston, JM "Irrigation as a solution to Agrarian Problems in Modern Spain" *The Geographical Journal*, Vol 116, July 1950

Munoz-Perez, JJ et al, "Cost of Beach Maintenance in the Gulf of Cádiz" *Coastal Engineering* 42, 2001 pp143-153

Tarazona, JV et al, "A Toxicological Assessment of Water Pollution and its Relationship to Aquaculture Development in Algeciras Bay, Cádiz, Spain" *Archives of Environmental Contamination and Toxicology* 20, 1991 pp480-487

Tremlett, G "Spain Buys up Coast to Halt Concrete Creep" *The Guardian* Sat September 16 2006

Politics

Harbon, JD "Spain, Spanish Morocco and Arab Policy" *African Affairs*, Vol 55, no. 219 April 1956

Conway, M "The politics and representation of disability in contemporary Spain" in Jordan, B Morgan-Tamosunas, R (eds.) *Contemporary Spanish Cultural Studies* (Arnold, London 2000)

17. Historic map - shifting field. 18. Historic map - ideal port city Francesco de Marchi (Della Architettura Militaire, 1599) 19. Historic map - sea battle. 20. Traders on the beach, Cádiz. Images: Archivo Historico Municipal de Cádiz

+work (landschaft)

saltcity Field+Work 2006-2008

In the essay, "Eidetic Operations and New Landscapes",[10] the landscape designer and theorist James Corner considers the relationship between landscape and image, bringing to the fore the notion of "landschaft" where the landscape is understood as neither innocent - natural - nor artifice - idea - but rather, space lived in time. He outlines a need for designers "to fully equip their arsenal of eidetic operations..."; their visual resources; the devices of close looking, recall, fabrication and imagination that distinguish the critical maker. He proposes a focus of attention on "the logic of making the landscape rather than its appearance per se".

"In the small-scale and sprawling inhabited landscape that surrounds even the most ordinary town in Europe, service industries have proliferated, laying down roots, finding a self-referential accommodation in a landscape that has lost its coherence...It requires of us a kind of tillage, a sifting to rediscover a landscape with critical properties. It requires us to sew into this landscape the beginnings of a new architecture which takes into consideration space, light and material scale: the specific mechanisms of place in relation to culture. In this landscape we are constantly tracing connections between strategy and detail in order to adjust our groundings and our views of the particular."[11]

Reniera fulva

Cacospongia scalaris

22

10 Corner, J ed. *Recovering Landscape: Essays in Contemporary Landscape Theory* (New York, Princeton Architectural Press, 2000) Chapter 10 pp153-169
11 Macdonald, C, Salter, P "Bespoke Territory" in Middleton, R ed. *The Idea of the City* (MIT Press, Cambridge, MA 1996)

The studio began with a research symposium, followed by an eight-day field trip to Cádiz. On return, students undertook a three-week design project for a *House for a Lookout* located in relation to the fortifications of the city. The symposium formulated a survey of themes and methods in order to create a discursive common ground. Fieldwork tools, guides and devices were consciously chosen as "the space of design"[12] shifted from Edinburgh to a less well-known (to us) territory. The journey between base and field and time away on the field trip allowed for getting lost, observing, collecting, recording, representing, collating, reading, measuring, acting in the city over time, a first version of understanding through working in the field.

Themes which aimed to situate the studio in a post-democracy political and cultural Spanish context included: the Bahia as a biological crossroads between Atlantic and Mediterranean flows; geological readings of the ground revealing ongoing macro scale material forces acting over time; the Islamic city, Recovery of Memory (1936 Spanish Civil War until 1975 Franco's death), tourist futures, Cádiz as strategic location, military and naval history, pollution/waste, spectacle, trauma and violence in Spanish culture. The Port was shown to be part of a very particular Mediterranean/North African network (Cremer). The southern coast of Spain was identified as porous, complicated by increasing flows of immigration (Perkin/Whitfield). Significant original fieldwork included the mapping of activity of the lively old Market, an experiment in rhythmanalysis[13] (Bush/Brooks), documentation of material porosity - ducts and air conditioning units - (Castle) and of water infrastructure (Fotheringham). A later archival study of Napoleonic action in the area demonstrated the sequential defensive containment of the urban core (Castle).

The controlling of access and egress to the field of the city has historically taken on a number of forms with related patterns of activity. One of the most visible was the eighteenth-century watchtower which occupied the rooftops of merchants' houses, enabling views oriented towards the harbour to watch for incoming ships/goods. These watchtowers interleave with the inhabited everyday fabric of the city. To some extent they become servant spaces, places of safety and withdrawal, yet with optical power and wider connection. This *landschaft*, urban field understood as space lived in time, was explored through design projects for a contemporary lookout house. Projects required an articulation of rationale for occupation, situation, arrangement, and logic of material consequence. Languages of design emerge - invented "idiolects" (a variety of a language unique to an individual) - which give permission to think and move. They become an eidetic operation of sorts, individual landscape narratives.

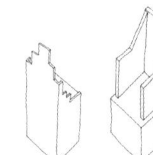 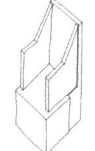 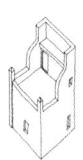 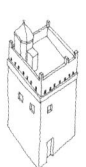 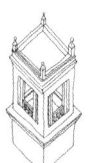 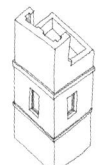 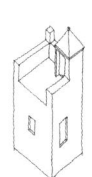 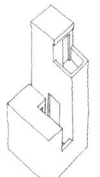  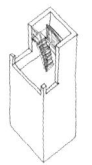 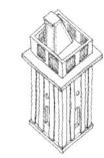 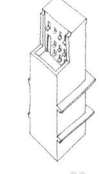

23

12 Wigley, M "Prosthetic Theory: The Disciplining of Architecture", *Assemblage* No.15 (Aug 1991) p20
13 Lefebvre, H "Rhythmanalysis of Mediterranean Cities" Kofman, E, Lebas, E eds *Henri Lefebvre: Writings on Cities* pp219-227

23. Typologies of watchtowers (Ross Perkin) 24. Port analysis (Annabel Cremer)

CHARACTERISTICS:

w, 36°3'N,
. WAVE HIGHT 5.50 M
. TIDE RANGE TIDE RANGE 3.90 M
RANCE CONDITIONS: 250 M WIDTH, 13 M DEPTH
A INNER ZONE (ENTRANCE, BASINS): 2800 M2
A OUTER ZONE II: 25.500 _TOTAL: 28.300 M2
RAGE AREA: 949.093 M2

LITIES:
` DOCKS
ATING DOCK
WAYS
YARD
RANES
HTHOUSES
EACONS (+42 PRIVATE)
IGHTED AIDS (+1 PRIVATE)
ND AID
S

PORT SANTA MARIA

PORT CABAZUELA

FREE ZONE

PORT OF BAY OF CADIZ

EISE

EGYPT

ITALY

MAROCCO

MAIN TRADE RELATIONS

FISHING BASIN
COMMERCIAL BASIN
FISHING QUAY
QUAY FOR OTHER USES
CONTAINER QUAY
PASSENGER

SHIP TRAFFIC.CADIZ. 2005
22.000/ YEAR
**5700 SPANISH
16,000 FOREIGN SHIPS
126.000 PASSENGERS**

SHIP ENTRY. TYPES.
**TANKERS 1200
BULK-CARGO
GERNERAL CARGO 2800
RO-RO 7084
PASSENGER 6200
CONTAINER 2500
OTHERS 300**

CADIZ TOTAL: 5,702,370
SPAIN TOTAL: 410,000,000
LONDON TOTAL: 53,000,000

GOODS TRAFFIC. CADIZ. 2005. TONS. CEREAL, FLOUR 904,000/ FRUITS, VEGETABLE 500,000/ METALL 427,000/ FOOD PRODUCTS 315,000/ COAL, PETROL COKE 240,000/ CANNED FOOD 144,000/ CHEMICAL PRODUCTS 116,000/ MACHINE EQUIP. 84,000/ ALCOHOL 81,000/ BUILDING MATERIAL 57,000/ OILS, GREASES 50,000/ ASPHALT 48,700/ TOBACCO, CACAO; COFFEE, SPICES 30,000/ FISH CAPTURE 26,200/ SOYA BEANS 15,000/ WOODS, CORK 21,000/ PAPER, WOOD PULP 20,000/ COMMOM SALT 4,600

Adam Collier *House for a Lookout* 2006

A key move in this project was the re-describing of the urban morphology as a geological landscape, which identified areas of potential weakness, fissure and previous consolidation. The *House for a Seismologist* investigated through drawings and models what might be at stake pragmatically and conceptually in engaging with the ground of Cádiz and the addition of weight and load at vulnerable points. The architectural proposal, the scale of inhabitation, is conceived as mediating a rupture identified at one of Cádiz's most dramatic changes in topography, an escarpment between the edge of the city on the Bahia and the lower ground where the main train route into the city is now located.

Emma Bush *House for a Lookout* 2006

The project is concerned with mapping the subtle topography of a part of the Old Town, researched on the field trip as a *Rhythmanalysist's Route*. Surmising it being flooded due to increasing global sea levels, a series of urban *salinas* (salt production pools) are proposed, inverting the urbanscape into a productive landscape. The proposal's arrangement and detail is underpinned by the daily and seasonal rhythms of tidal flows exploring how a salina gatekeeper would interact with and dwell within this new topography.

ednesday 13th September 2006

nrise	8.05 am
nset	8.36 pm
n tide	1.20 am
tide	7.33 am
n tide	1.42 pm
tide	7.54pm
length	11h 31m
onphase	14
nperature	25 degrees
nfall	0mm
d	4mph NW

00 am	close gate 3
30 am	open gate 1
40-2.50 am	sleep - lookout in Teatro Genoves
0 am	close gate 1
0-6.40 am	sleep - lookout in Teatro Genoves
0 am	open gate 5
0 am	control gate series 6
0-9.50am	rest and breakfast - Baluarte De Candelaria
00 am	open gate 4
30 am	herd fish through gate 2
00 am	open gate 3
20 am	take fish from fish garden to boats - taken to market
50 am	close gate 3
00 pm	open gate 1
0-3.20pm	lunch and free time - Teatro Genoves
0 pm	close gate 1
0-9.00 pm	work in salt gardens - raking pans, piling salt, processing and packing
30 pm	open gate 4
00 pm	herd fish through gate 2
30 pm	open gate 3
20 am	close gate 3
40 am	open gate 1
50-3.00am	sleep - lookout in Teatro Genoves

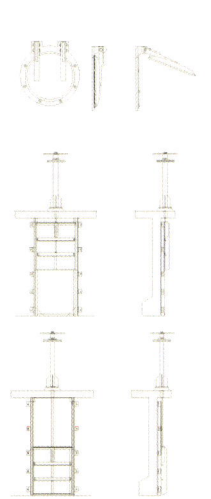

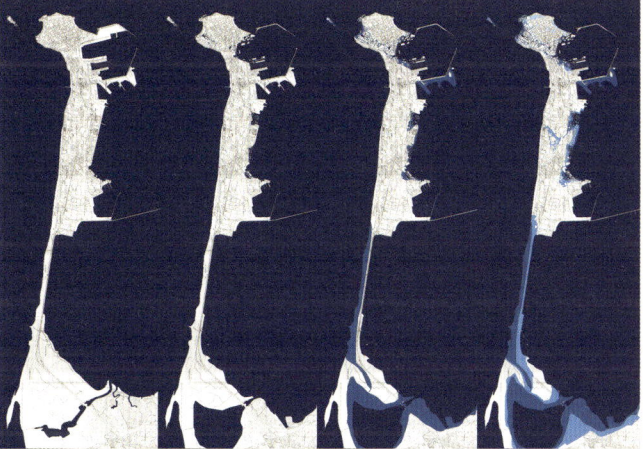

Mike Whitfield *House for a Lookout* 2006

Research established the coast of southwestern Spain as porous and problematic in terms of contemporary movements of people, predominantly from Africa to Europe, south to north. While Cádiz has historically been a portal for flows of goods, people and ideas through trade, war and national consolidation, the current condition seems to be an outworking of globalisation and centres on economic migrancy with significant urban consequences. Precise recording of the spatial and temporal movement of an immigrant umbrella seller before, during and after short rainfalls, was the starting point for conceiving of a House for a Lookout located on a roof overlooking the main market, where temporary stalls can be set up within minutes of potential customers appearing.

Annabel Cremer *House for a Lookout* 2006

Concerns were focused on the immediate territory of the Port of Cádiz, a considerable site on the international trade route since the Phoenician Empire, and defined through the notion of displacement. The tightly prescribed peninsular condition of the city is read as a constant flow of arrival, exchange, consumption and waste. At the scale of intimate provision, the path of a fish from line to plate via market stall was traced for an individual resident of the Old Town, revealing particular characteristics and resistances of the urban ground, and potential strategies for containment while in motion.

Cardea, Roman goddess of - amongst other things - door hinges
"her power is to open what is shut; to shut what is open."[14]

hinge 1

25. The Cádiz City Plan installed in Studio 5, Edinburgh. Image: Robert Willis
26. CCPO Programmers plotting individual projects. Image: Mike Whitfield

During the course of the *Cádiz Field+Work* studio two group projects proved critical to the development of working practices and thematic content. The first hinge (project), *The Cádiz City Plan(ning) Office [CCPO]* took place between the initial individual territorial claims of fieldwork and desk research of Semester 1 and the strategic city and spatial design work of Semester 2.

This eight-day project was an exploration of "performative architectural education". Thirty-two students (including eight MSc Advanced Architectural Design students) participated, working with 2006-2007 Visiting Simpson Professor of Architecture, Ben Nicholson, and programme tutors, Suzanne Ewing and Victoria Clare Bernie. The brief for the *CCPO* was to work together to collate and consolidate the thirty-two territories and themes identified so far by each student. *The Cádiz City Plan* was presented at 1pm on Thursday, 18 January 2007 in Studio 5, 20 Chambers Street, Edinburgh to Professors Ben Nicholson and Andrew Benjamin. The *CCPO* established a matrix of relationships where projects were initially plotted on a graph with x-axis *elysian-apocalyptic*, and y-axis *self-sufficiency-dependency*.

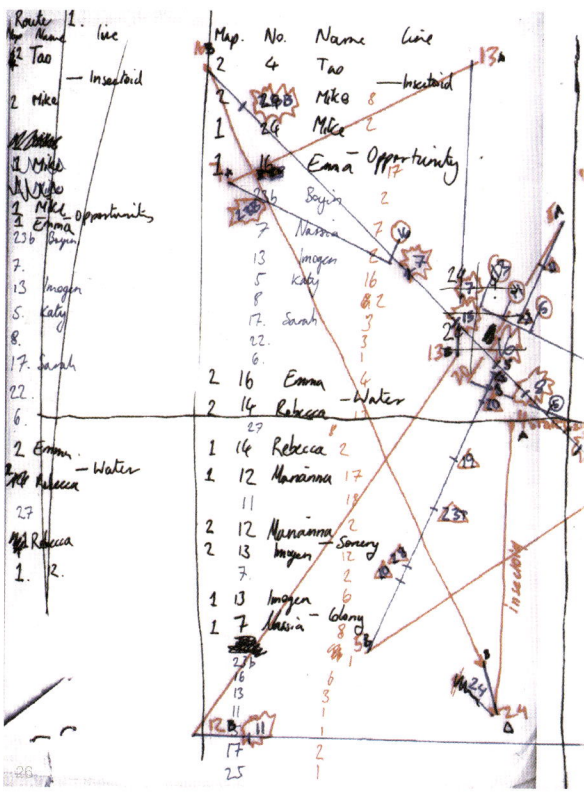

"How a group of people choreograph themselves and motivate themselves is probably the most difficult challenge of large group projects. The matter of who is in charge or apparently telling people what to do, whose ideas you use, whose ideas you don't use and who goes to buy the coffee are issues that become more and more insurmountable the larger the group becomes…personal ego was an impossibility in the project because so many people had ownership in having touched the ideas at some point."

Andrew Brooks

14 *"numine clausa aperit, claudit aperta suo"*, Littlewood, R J A *Commentary on Ovid: Fasti Book VI* (Oxford University Press, Oxford, 2006) p40

Individual student responses to "What went on in the *CCPO*?", completed shortly after the project, and a paper by the Programme Organiser, serve to demonstrate a rich range of new understandings of the potentiality and the contingent nature of collective practice.[15] In acknowledging conditions of urban temporality and connective failure in the city, the project disclosed new ways of imagining and engaging with its complexities, processes and logics for action.

Hinge 1 acknowledges the moving backwards/forwards/through of the architectural design process. A possibility that distinguishes the relative generosity of a two-year studio-based programme. The work produced raises questions of collective and individual design practice(s) and relationships between research, fieldwork and design. It draws attention to teaching architectural design as a process that operates between exercise and experiment. An enlarged photographic image from the final installation, *Film 1: Making the CCPO*, and *Film 2: Performing the CCPO*, was exhibited in the Royal Scottish Academy Student Exhibition 2007.[16]

"Each of the 32 class members could point to the part that *is* them…It is about anonymity, about questioning self, questioning where one idea begins or ends or overlaps or becomes simultaneously multiples and one."

Emma Bush

15 Ewing, S "Experimenting with a performative project: The Cádiz City Plan(ning) Office" *Teaching and Experimenting with Architectural Design: Advances in Technology and Changes in Pedagogy* (ENHSA-EAAE Transactions in Architectural Education no 35, Thessaloniki, Greece, 2008)
16 Illustrated in RSA *Student Exhibition 2007 Catalogue* p.14. Exhibit no. 20 (Sculpture Court)

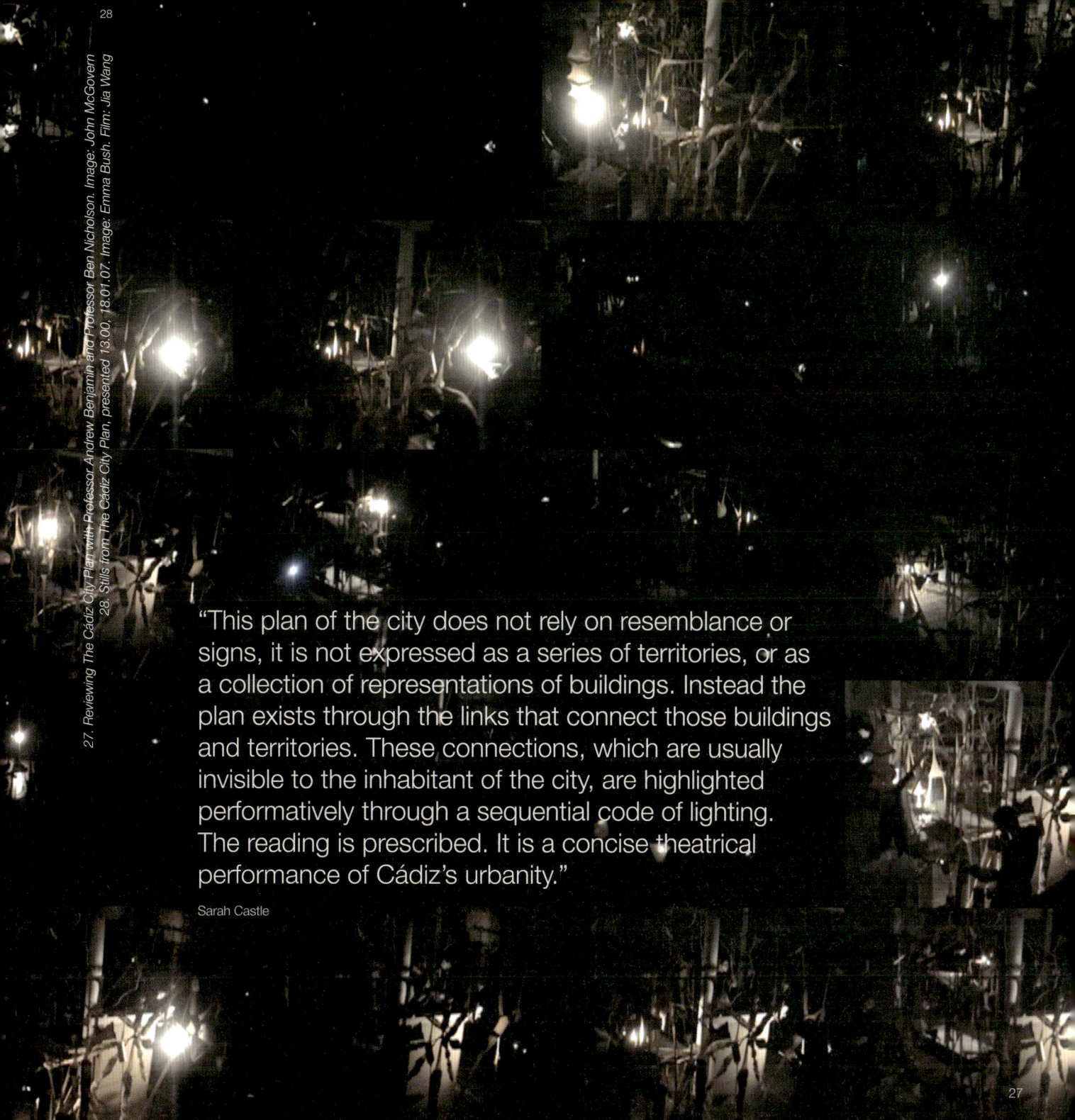

27. Reviewing The Cádiz City Plan with Professor Andrew Benjamin and Professor Ben Nicholson. Image: John McGovern
28. Stills from The Cádiz City Plan, presented 13.00, 18.01.07. Image: Emma Bush. Film: Jia Wang

"This plan of the city does not rely on resemblance or signs, it is not expressed as a series of territories, or as a collection of representations of buildings. Instead the plan exists through the links that connect those buildings and territories. These connections, which are usually invisible to the inhabitant of the city, are highlighted performatively through a sequential code of lighting. The reading is prescribed. It is a concise theatrical performance of Cádiz's urbanity."

Sarah Castle

"The Greek work mēchanē ('machine') is frequently used in contexts connected with irrigation…"[17]

+work (mēchanē)

29. Thesis projects installed in studio, May 2007. Image: Victoria Clare Bernie

30. Motions of the City: Institutional leisure and dreamtime studies (Annabel Cremer, Adam Collier, Claire Goodsell). Image: Adam Collier

In his general introduction to *The Practice of Everyday Life* Michel de Certeau sets out his urban project: "a continuing investigation of the ways in which users…operate." His observations concern firstly, ways of *being* in the city through "readers' practices, practices related to urban spaces, utilisations of everyday rituals, re-uses and functions of the memory through: the 'authorities' that make possible (or permit) everyday practices…" and secondly, ways of *acting* in the city through: "trajectories", "tactics" and "rhetorics", "reading", "talking", "dwelling", "cooking".

Such a close unpacking of the city as a ground for operations serves both the student and the educator. Applied to the study city - a relatively or completely unknown ground - it offers both tools for action and clues for interpretation and, in doing so, it avoids prescription: the city for operations is a lived entity, existing in time. The project of an urban understanding is always self-consciously contingent.

All design projects are to some extent versions of de Certeau's "wandering line": staged investigations, unplanned adventures, pragmatic descriptions, sketches, drafts, proofs, remarkable schemes and ridiculous fictions. For the student, the programme and the brief can identify the field without prescribing a means of operation whilst the further discourse of the tutorial, the review, the collective and the individual project can help to chart the journey. We talk a lot in the studio of tracing the path of design practice, being able to track moves in order to provide opportunities to re-enter or manipulate "out of" sequence.

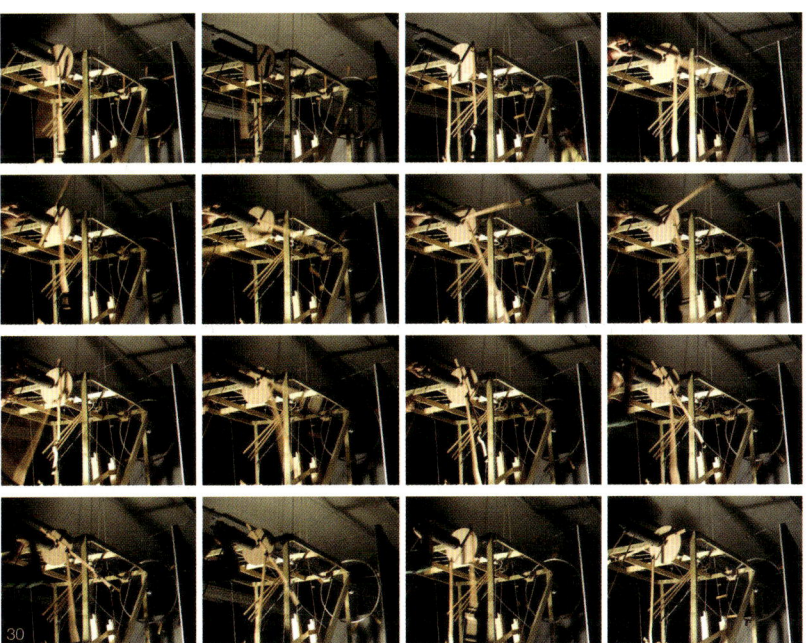

30

17 Landels, JG "Engineering in the Ancient World" (Constable, London, 1998) p59

The professionalisation of architectural design necessarily pushes design practice towards the fundamentally strategic, operating within the constraining orders of financial formulae and frameworks, city control, governance, legislation and risk management. In this studio students are exposed to more tactical ways of operating. Placing the "making" of architecture as part of a larger understanding of cultural "making" of cities is intentional and aims to provoke a critical engagement with future modes of architectural (professional) practice. Students of architectural design are generally tactical in their initial engagements with a study city, they therefore operate with "tact": precisely, opportunistically and in direct relation to instant, circumstance and "making do", using tricks and tenacity.

Donald Schön has argued that the design studio has shifted from problem solving to problem setting.[18] The question posed at the start of the Cádiz Design Thesis was "What does the City (Metropolitan area of Cádiz) need (desire)?" This exposed the studio to complexity, who articulates city futures, and how many possible futures are there? The teaching practice of the studio was positioned:

- City (urbanism) is a rich but contested domain which requires further scrutiny and critical analysis.

- New and appropriate architectural possibilities can be uncovered and developed through strategies used to "uncover" or reveal the city itself (performative, diagnostic, empirical, metaphorical…)

- Despite current debate about the deterritorialisation of architecture, we can learn and act most precisely as architects through continuing engagement with the specific and the particular, rather than the generic or universal.

- Critical making is a productive method of architectural analysis.

"Thesis" was introduced as an active term, a proposition related to city which is explored and developed over time. It is a demonstration of personal position uncovered through research in field and studio, testing, design proposal and reflective analysis.

"The city has lost the balance needed to maintain itself."
Katie Nicolson

18 Schön, DA. *The design studio: an exploration of its traditions and potentials* (RIBA Publications for RIBA Building Industry Trust, London, 1985)

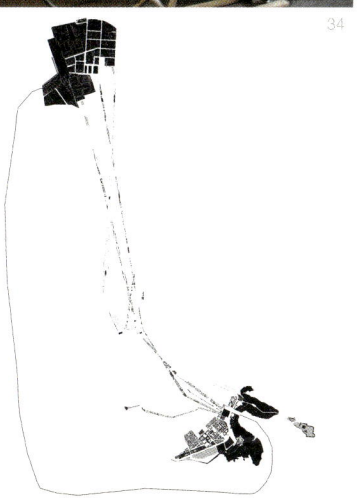

31. Construction site, Cádiz. Image: Mike Whitfield. 32. Spatial Strategy: Shifted, locked city (Adam Collier, Claire Goodsell)
33. City Strategy: City Locking Machine - (Annabel Cremer, Adam Collier, Claire Goodsell). Image: John McGovern. 34. Spatial Strategy Shiftmap (Adam Collier)

The timing and pacing of work during the Design Thesis was carefully choreographed. A two-week group project, *City Strategy*, aimed to establish the multiplicity of layers that constitute Cádiz through critical making and active archiving. The work made included: a Reinforcement/failure map, a Locking Machine, Friction Devices, a Time/Fortune Machine, Clamp/Hinge/Lift tools, a Sticky territory map, a Guide to fear, Daedalus' Ducts (Infrastructural Labyrinth), a Gap reading machine, a Self-sufficiency game. Overarching paradoxes emerged: a city of material tactics and spatial disconnections, a peri-urban metropolitan network with a fundamentally pedestrian grain, a city of contested environments.

Spatial strategy (field actions) tested the consequences of City Strategy, tackling issues of site, scale, production and operation consolidating in a collective exhibition which transformed working studios into a place of display. If the city is a context needing or desiring some sort of irrigation (physical, cultural, political, social, economic), mēchanē ("machine") can be seen in relation to the design process: where the efficient mechanic (architect acting in the city) develops skill over time, gains knowledge of parts, and enables smooth running, synchronisation, timing and performance. Potential mēchanē (as irrigating actions) include naming, limiting/extending, enclosing/filtering, material scribing/displacing, threshold control/fluidity, spatial sequencing/repetition/rhythm, logics of part-to-whole.

Scales of Enquiry explored the operation of design propositions at 1: global, 1:1000, 1:100 and 1:local scale aiming to develop working practices which engender design agility. Urban scale moves were tested through fragments created at a more experientially legible scale. Fragments were tested through maps, drawings and construction represented at a "distance". *Elaboration* was a detailed enquiry into what constitutes the appropriate technological responses to a brief, expressed through the exploration of construction, material, structure, environment and sustainable response. Issues emerged as particularly pertinent to Cádiz: the microclimate of the urban grain - air and water flows, thermal mass and cooling, shelter from wind and sea; the ecological fragility of the coast in contest with historic pollution/pollutants; degrees of energy/material self-sufficiency or dependency; landscape/production infrastructures and associated historic techniques - irrigation, hydraulics, salt extraction; local-global material supply and manufacture; the politics and flow of immigrant construction workers in the region. A dedicated period of research aimed to inform the Thesis projects in profound and unexpected ways. In closing, Thesis work was articulated in a documented, installed exhibition.

35

"…most interesting to us was the idea of the underground labyrinth under the city, created by Daedalus, master craftsman…It is in this way that we devised our model of an understanding of Cádiz, we wanted to model an understanding of various infrastructural systems and how they fit together in the city. This produces a labyrinthine system when immersed within the model, but when viewed with more perspective the overall logic is apparent."

Andrew Brooks, Sarah Castle

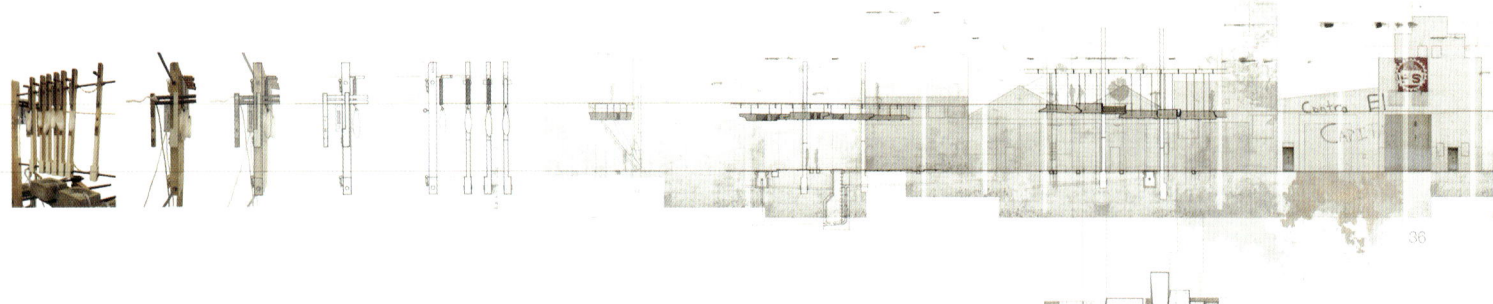

36

35. City Strategy: Infrastructural Labyrinth (Andrew Brooks, Sarah Castle). 36. Spatial Strategy: Cortadura Infrastructure (Sarah Castle). 37. City Strategy: Reinforcement/failure map (Emma Bush, Ross Perkin, Sofi Tegsveden).

"February 5th.

Today was the day we went for it. We took the risks that we'd been talking about and poured bucketfuls of sloppy liquid into a thin piece of fabric pinned within a wobbly frame suspended above the ground. And it worked. We had added various strings, struts and cables, but as the thing was bending and distorting at every opportunity, what had been tightly tensioned became slack. As we tethered New Town to the (now reinstated) Torregorda, Old Town slumped and buckled, and the Port gained increased supporting prominence in order to counter this action. The actual pour was frantic, and although plaster lapped and dripped over the edges, creating a city form (shadow?) on the ground beneath, there was no point of absolute breach (there was one occasion when an additional makeshift support had to be hurriedly implemented) and all in all we considered it an anti-failure!"

Emma Bush, Sofi Tegsveden, Ross Perkin

Jie Lin *Migrant Landscape* 2007

The city of Cádiz is dense and compact and appears to be saturated. Based on fieldwork observation and data analysis, migrant colonisation and urban circulation were starting points for the project. How can urban property be changed to meet the needs of an increasing transitory population, while the resident population of the city is declining? Any intervention requires spatial renegotiation of the existing saturated condition. This renegotiation has been investigated through devices, tools and projects looking for, adjusting and occupying physical and programmatic gaps in the city: image analysis, G-clamp, de-laminating drawn and modelled information. The urban rescripting of a *Migrant Landscape*, and a relocated *Law Court*.

clamping

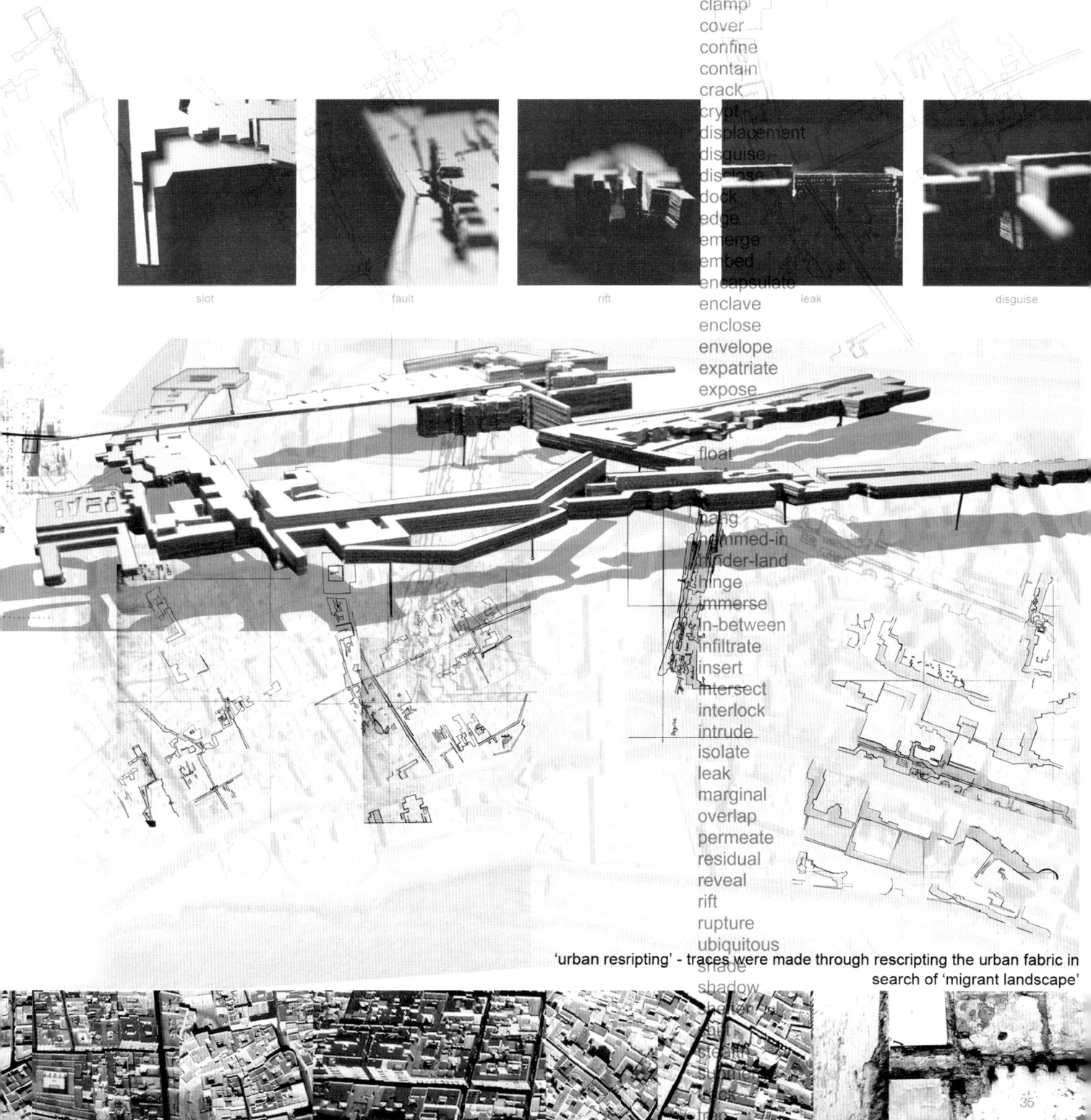

slot

fault

rift

leak

disguise

clamp
cover
confine
contain
crack
crypt
displacement
disguise
disclose
dock
edge
emerge
embed
encapsulate
enclave
enclose
envelope
expatriate
expose

float

hang
hemmed-in
hinder-land
hinge
immerse
in-between
infiltrate
insert
intersect
interlock
intrude
isolate
leak
marginal
overlap
permeate
residual
reveal
rift
rupture
ubiquitous
shade
shadow

steal
submer
back

'urban resripting' - traces were made through rescripting the urban fabric in search of 'migrant landscape'

35

Mike Whitfield *Manifestations of an un-Official Minority (Non-Citizen's Advice Bureau)* 2007

Research revealed individual narratives of economic migrants moving through Cádiz, and exposed a temporal and spatial limbo between physical arrival and official acknowledgement as an asylum seeker or immigrant. The notion of the urban fabric being integral to and an expression of the collectivity of official citizens is called into question. Migrants bring skills, registers of other grains of cities, in this case, Islamic, and associated civic behaviours, as well as needs: employment, networks and community. A *Non-Citizen's Advice Bureau* is tested as a semi-official locus, while the slim space of a street door recess is adapted to enable a *Tailor* to offer his services. Emerging material/fabric metaphors are contingent on an implicitly more expansive setting: seam, veil, thread, weave.

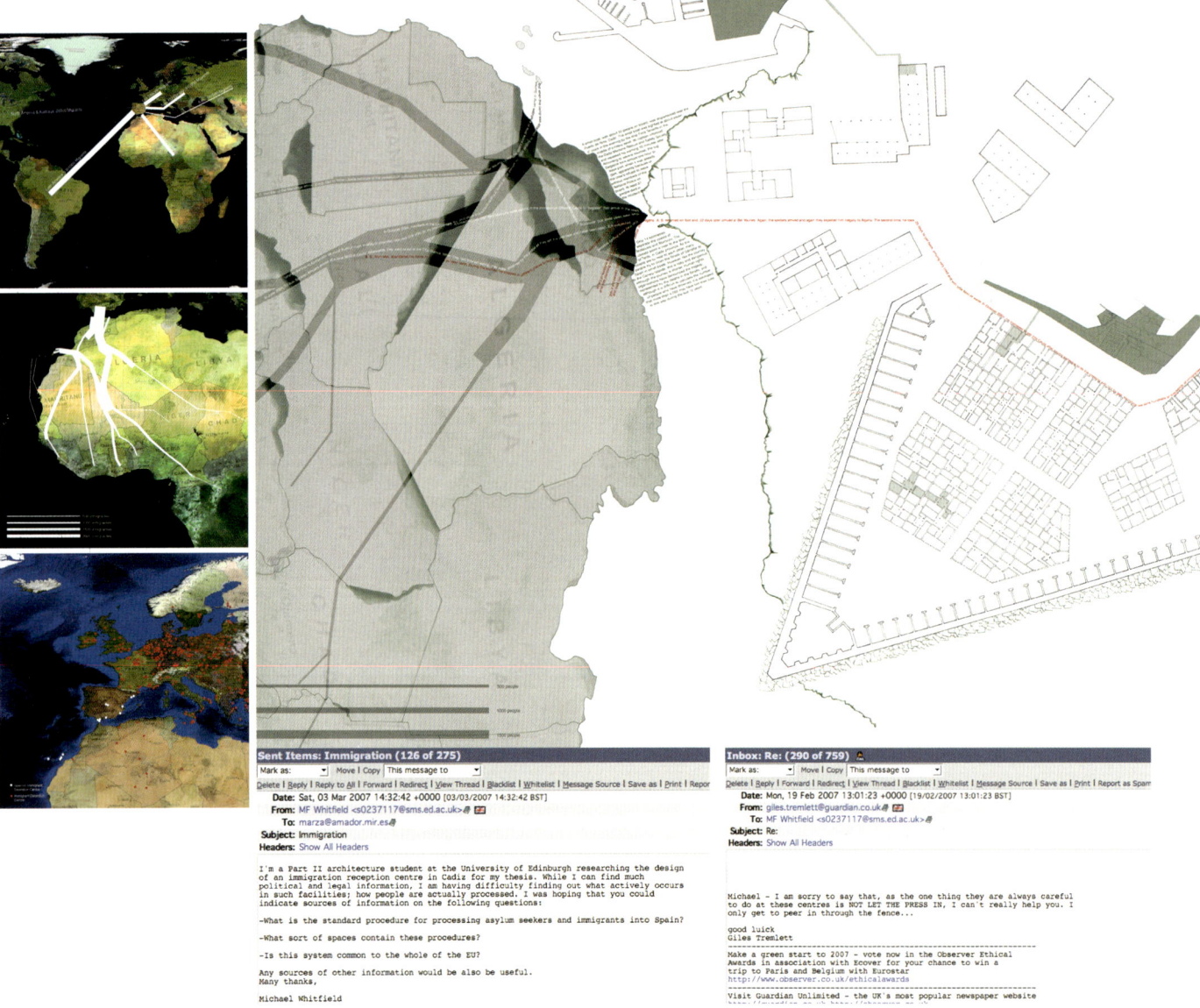

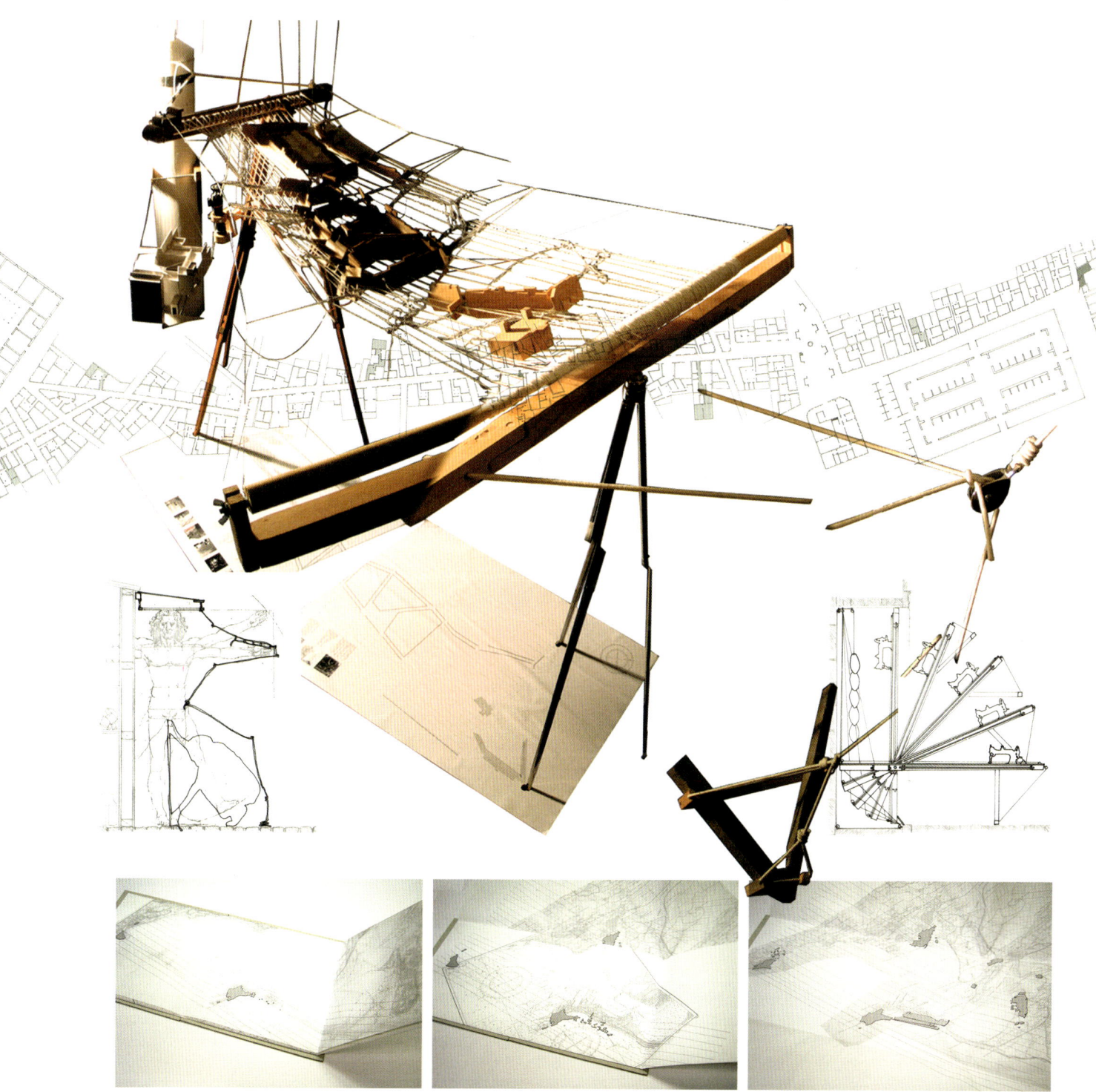

Annabel Cremer *Value: Displacement over Space and Time* 2007

The project sought to formulate an approach to designing in Cádiz as a condition of urban flow, where the matter of the city operated in a continuous process of exchange. The displacement of matter is acknowledged from the macro-scale of twenty-four hour international shipping to the micro-scale of opportunistic, peri-legal barter. The distillation of site, action and material is explored in a proposal for a *Universal Stock Exchange* for Cádiz capable of acknowledging the immediacy of the almost legal street barter, and the abstraction of the almost legal international monetary markets. Can and should architecture register any notion of value within its design? What definition of value might be represented?

Sarah Castle *Cortadura: the Cut City* 2007

A Sand Duct proposal explored the differentiation of the Bay and Atlantic edges of Cádiz, suggesting that public routes set against the main traffic grain could be accentuated through physical augmentation of the ground. This also raised questions of the limit of the city, shifting concern to the Zona de la Cortadura, an industrial area near the remnant of a Napoleonic fort. The project consolidates a glossary of "cuts" which are assembled and re-interpreted at various points of urban resistance, suggesting particular ways of intervening with the ground. A series of bridges explore the consequence of a literal "thickening" of the ground. How might a new public infrastructure and framework for inhabitation be introduced, acknowledging the need for critical action in this typically sprawling, slippery urban landscape?

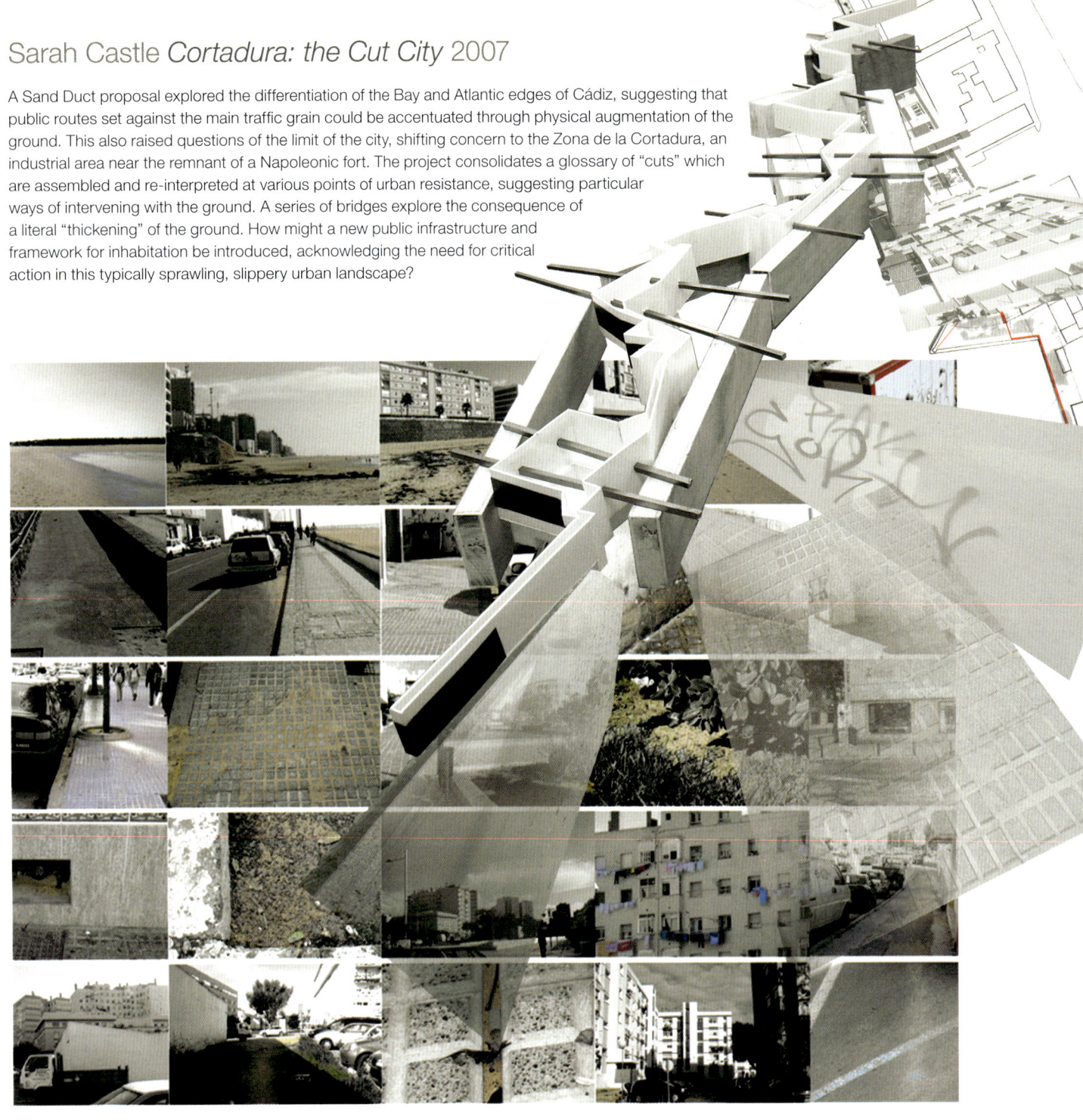

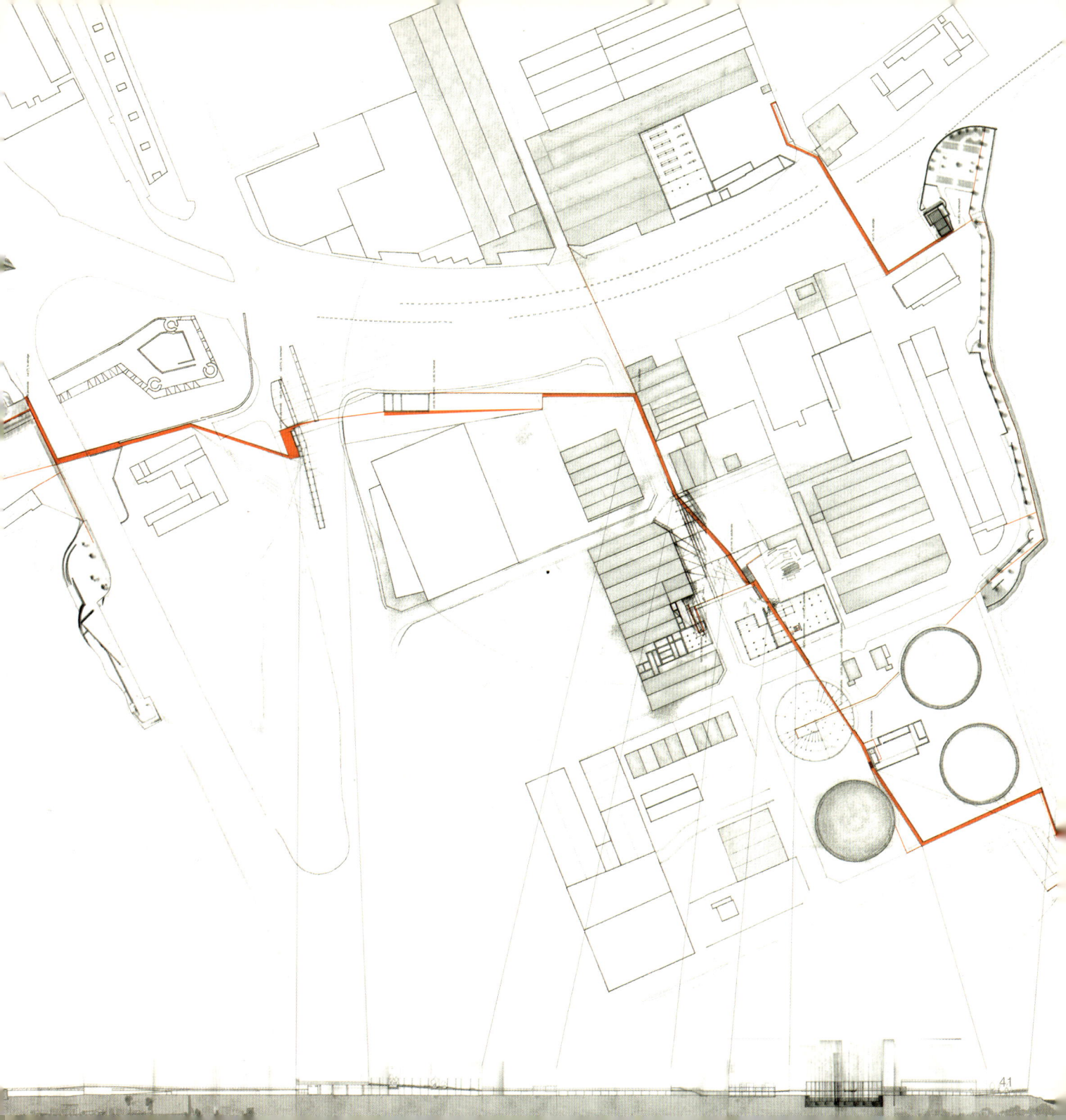

hinge, n. a type of bearing that connects two solid objects, typically allowing only a limited angle of rotation between them[19]

hinge 2

saltcity Field+Work 2006-2008

Hinge 2, The Cádiz City Model [CCM] enabled choreographed movement between individual design propositions in empirical sites in Cádiz and the fabrication of a reassembled urban field as the context for concluding thesis projects in the closing months of the programme.

This twelve-day project took place in the second year of the programme, working with programme tutors, Suzanne Ewing and Victoria Clare Bernie. The brief for the CCM was to work together to construct twenty-three ongoing architectural propositions on their sites and in relationship to each other at 1:500 scale, utilising a considered, well-crafted urban armature, and a visual field archive. *The Cadiz City Model* was launched at 8pm on Tuesday, 22 January 2008 (almost precisely one year after the *CCPO* presentation) in Studio 4, 20 Chambers Street, Edinburgh to an audience of invited students, tutors and visitors. An informal presentation was made to 2008-2009 Visiting Simpson Professor of Architecture, Iñaki Abalos.

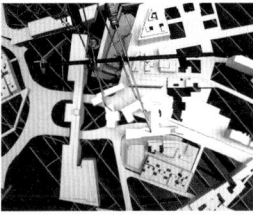

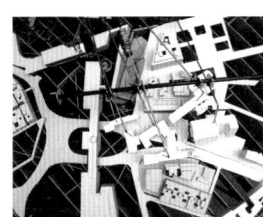

39

"...it makes twenty-three versions of a fiction solid. As if twenty-three authors were trying to write the same book at the same time. Some characters may be straightforward, if only one person is concerned with that section of the story. Others may be more complex, positioning a system of collaboration, over- and re-writing...Collectively we learnt exactly what is meant by *our* Cádiz. What its extents are, where its borders fade to nothing, or where they butt up precisely against another."

Emma Bush

19 Oxford English Dictionary (Oxford University Press, Oxford, 2008)

"*The Cádiz City Model* works well in the studio, and really gives an impression of the shape/topography/density…as well as a sense of arrival/entry to the city from the elevated vantage of the stairs of the studio, drawing the visitor into *our* world of Cádiz."

Andrew Mackie

Individual student responses to "What was made in the *CCM*?", completed shortly after the project, demonstrate a confidence arising from the augmentation of collective practice begun in the *CCPO [Hinge 1]*, a collective authorship in dialogue with a deepened understanding of individual propositions and the potential for new relationships with other projects. *Hinge 2* might be understood as an acting out of the moving backwards/forwards/through of the architectural design process. The 2006-2008 studio was "petrified" as a consolidation of the collective territorial moves. The empirical anchor became mediated, a material manifestation in grey card, black steel, black thread, uplight and projected film footage. The potential of the territory had been "realized". The studio's understanding of the field belonging to the city was demonstrated through the positioned armature and its relationship to the territory above; the datum calibration of the grey card sections, the grey card registration of relevant 1:500 urban morphology, and the cumulative acts of irrigation of individual design proposals. These used the model context as a new anchor, an interpretative one, which engendered new readings, speculations and generative possibilities.

"A consistency of material and technique of everybody's separate modelling projects allows for a very real scrutiny across the city; this is also facilitated by the common ownership."

Andrew Brooks

40. The 'Cádiz City Model' launch, January 2008. Image: Rachel Travers
41. The 'Cádiz City Model' launch, January 2008. Image: Rob Willis Euan Cockburn, Emma Bush

"Opportunities arise from conversations, often with the appearance of argument - ideas are worked through and questioned, taken apart and put back together...Contrastingly, compromise is often achieved when people do not question. It is either the moment when someone relents or it is the moment when people have apparently agreed, done something in the meantime, come back together and found they no longer "fit" and have to be pushed together in the way that both parties are least uncomfortable with...There is a point when someone needs to relent or something needs to be made."

Michael Whitfield

"Most importantly, school has to teach the future architect the elements of praxis: how to speak properly, how to articulate a position…"[20]

+work (praxis)

saltcity Field+Work 2006-2008

How does an architect gain knowledge of the city and learn how to use this as a basis for critical practice? Architecture School can provide the time and pedagogical frameworks to develop and make manifest the processes of practice, preparing future architects for more "indeterminate zones" where product is privileged. To speak "properly" - thoughtfully, with self-awareness, tact and confidence - through skills of text, drawing, model, exhibition, film, verbal communication. To "articulate a position" - to have a clear understanding of relevant disciplinary knowledge, knowledge of macro and micro forces active in an urban field, ability to identify and analyse limits and constraints, and to know how to begin acting as an architect.

Through the theme of *Field+Work*, the Cádiz Studio 2006-2008 has cultivated original research practice, developed a distinctive pedagogical philosophy, and explored iterative relationships between research and design. The studio has produced rich, sensitive, thoughtful architectural proposals positioned in a particular urban field with the potential to unfold over time. *SaltCity* can be seen as a possible trajectory of cities of the slow economy that acknowledges temporal aspects of urbanism, suggests thoughtful and detailed scrutiny, and puts forward tactics of engagement with inventive conceptual and pragmatic techniques.

20 Pérez-Gómez, A "Architecture and Ethics Beyond Globalization" ARCC/EAAE Montreal Conference on Architectural Research eds Fontein, L, Neukerman, H (Belgium, 2001) pp13-22

Engagement with particular resistances of the field of the metropolitan area of Cádiz includes scrutinising spatial grain, disjunctions, tensions. Four main fields of Cádiz have been worked with - the Old Town, New Town, Port and Spanned Territories. Concerns which have emerged in the studio range in scale from infrastructural networks to intimate urban moments. Culminating proposals are based on personal research, outcomes of individual design project testings, and knowledge and strategies gained from the collective endeavours of the studio over twenty months.

In *Landscapes and Production: Cultivating a Biotechnological Field in the Bay of Cádiz*, **Emma Bush** explores Architecture as a calibrating, irrigating and incubating agent in the Darsena de Atilleros dry dock. **Rebecca Fotheringham**'s research into landscapes of water management in southern Spain, and reading of Cádiz as a Hydropolis, has underpinned her proposals for a series of buildings between the Cathedral and Town Hall in the Old Town, *Hydroscape: the Hydropolitical Strand*. A new commercial district just outside the Puerta de Tierra - old city gate - is proposed by **Adam Collier** in *Re-programming the Ruptured City.* His work in this area has stemmed from understandings of projected geological activity and a particular concern with places of rupture that may catalyse opportunities for new urban inhabitation, and may provide a logic for urban and architectural arrangement. Since the extension of the New Town in the twentieth century, the City edge has drifted and dissolved into beach/freeway/industrial zone. **Sarah Castle** in *The Vesselled City: Precipitating Human Activity at the City Edge*, has been working with this common contemporary urban condition and how it may be re-anchored through urban grain and residential use. Statistics uncovered on the flow of immigrants alongside narratives which reveal needs and desires not able to be met explicitly by a civic authority has driven *Secreted Seams: Wanderings and Fabrics in Old Town Cádiz* by **Mike Whitfield**. Can Architecture be imagined as a series of connected urban moments which may engender transcultural encounters and an enriched public life? **Jie Lin** in *Threshold…Innerspace…Space Behind…Hidden Space* also explores what role Architecture - as intervention in existing urban fabric - might play in augmenting the experience of transient populations. **Ross Perkin**'s proposals for *El Ciné de las Torres (New Worlds within the Old Town of Cádiz)* are literally grounded in the speculative archaeological remains of a Roman circus, and explore how cinema, film and defined public routes may reinforce a decaying part of the city conceptually, materially and experientially.

45&46. Cádiz, 2006. Images: Victoria Clare Bernie. 47. Marine calibration (Annabel Cremer) 48. Napoleonic seige: consolidated map (Sarah Castle)

Other Thesis Design and Research Projects for the City completed in Year 2:

David Ambrose: *Activating the City: Protocols for a Sustainable Urban Coast*

Andrew Brooks: *Mutable Spaces and Infrastucture*

Emma Bush/Sarah Castle/Adam Collier: *BioCity*

Eric Chen: *Hinging Seam*

Euan Cockburn: *Mural Frontier*

Wen Foo: *Rhythmic Assemblage, Heterotopic City*

Claire Goodsell: *Resistance and Erosion of Urban Coast*

Imogen Hogg: *Towards an Autotrophic City*

Craig Hutchinson: *Re-entering the City: Cádiz in Friction*

Jessica Ji: *Dilating Edge*

Andrew Mackie: *(Sea) Gate*

Kate Nicholson: *Microsurgery, Ossiointegration and the Taphonomic Boundary*

Cory Wang: *Host/Guest*

Tao Wang: *Drifting Field*

Robert Willis: *City of Friction*

Tong Wu: *Augmented Boundaries*

Boyin Yang: *Shifting Boundaries in the Mechanism City*

Architectural production in the *Cádiz Field+Work* Studio 2006-2008 has been characterised by an openness to collaborative exploration, a rigour of operation, documentation, making and re-making. The work of the studio has probably come closest to engagement with the contested complexity of the urban project when operating on the margins of the conventional academic arena: when "out of place" during a field trip and fieldwork or when operating collectively, experimenting in Year 1 with a project to construct a City Plan, and in Year 2, when constructing a propositional City Model. Each instance draws attention to the shortcomings of single-vision projects or Architecture as solely product or object. The co-existence and proximities of the strategic (overview, collective city operations) with the tactical (individual excursions and diversions) allows necessary responsiveness of shifting research strategies and tactics that may deepen the transformative potential of both Field and Work in Architecture.

47

48

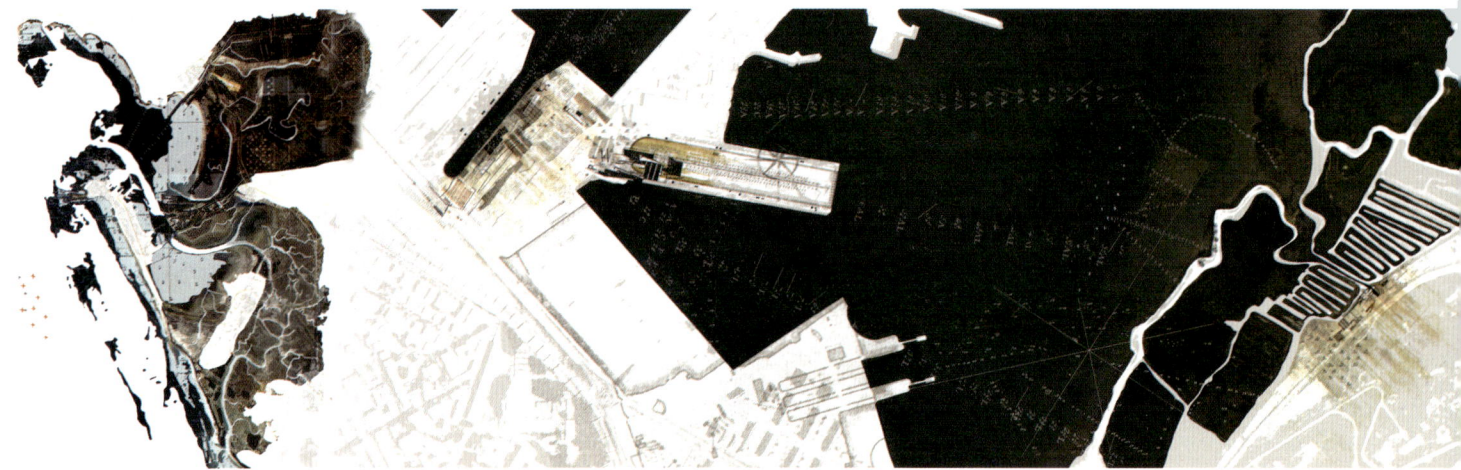

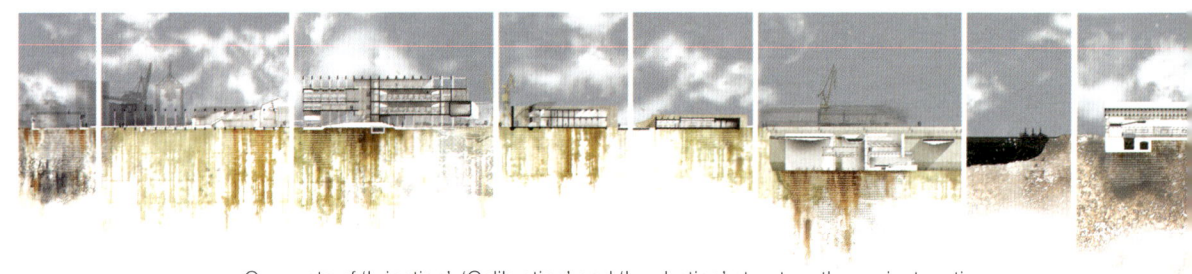

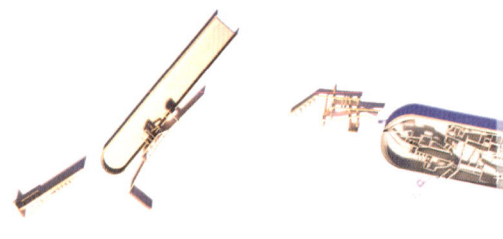

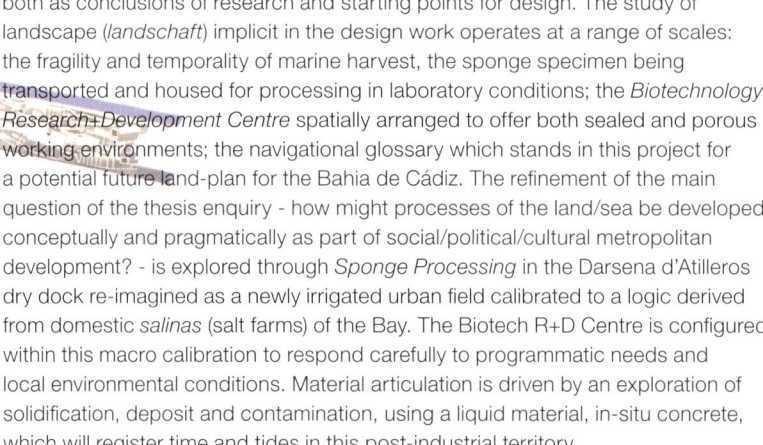

Concepts of 'Irrigation', 'Calibration' and 'Incubation' structure the project, acting both as conclusions of research and starting points for design. The study of landscape (*landschaft*) implicit in the design work operates at a range of scales: the fragility and temporality of marine harvest, the sponge specimen being transported and housed for processing in laboratory conditions; the *Biotechnology Research+Development Centre* spatially arranged to offer both sealed and porous working environments; the navigational glossary which stands in this project for a potential future land-plan for the Bahia de Cádiz. The refinement of the main question of the thesis enquiry - how might processes of the land/sea be developed conceptually and pragmatically as part of social/political/cultural metropolitan development? - is explored through *Sponge Processing* in the Darsena d'Atilleros dry dock re-imagined as a newly irrigated urban field calibrated to a logic derived from domestic *salinas* (salt farms) of the Bay. The Biotech R+D Centre is configured within this macro calibration to respond carefully to programmatic needs and local environmental conditions. Material articulation is driven by an exploration of solidification, deposit and contamination, using a liquid material, in-situ concrete, which will register time and tides in this post-industrial territory.

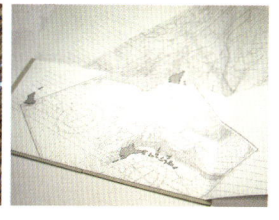

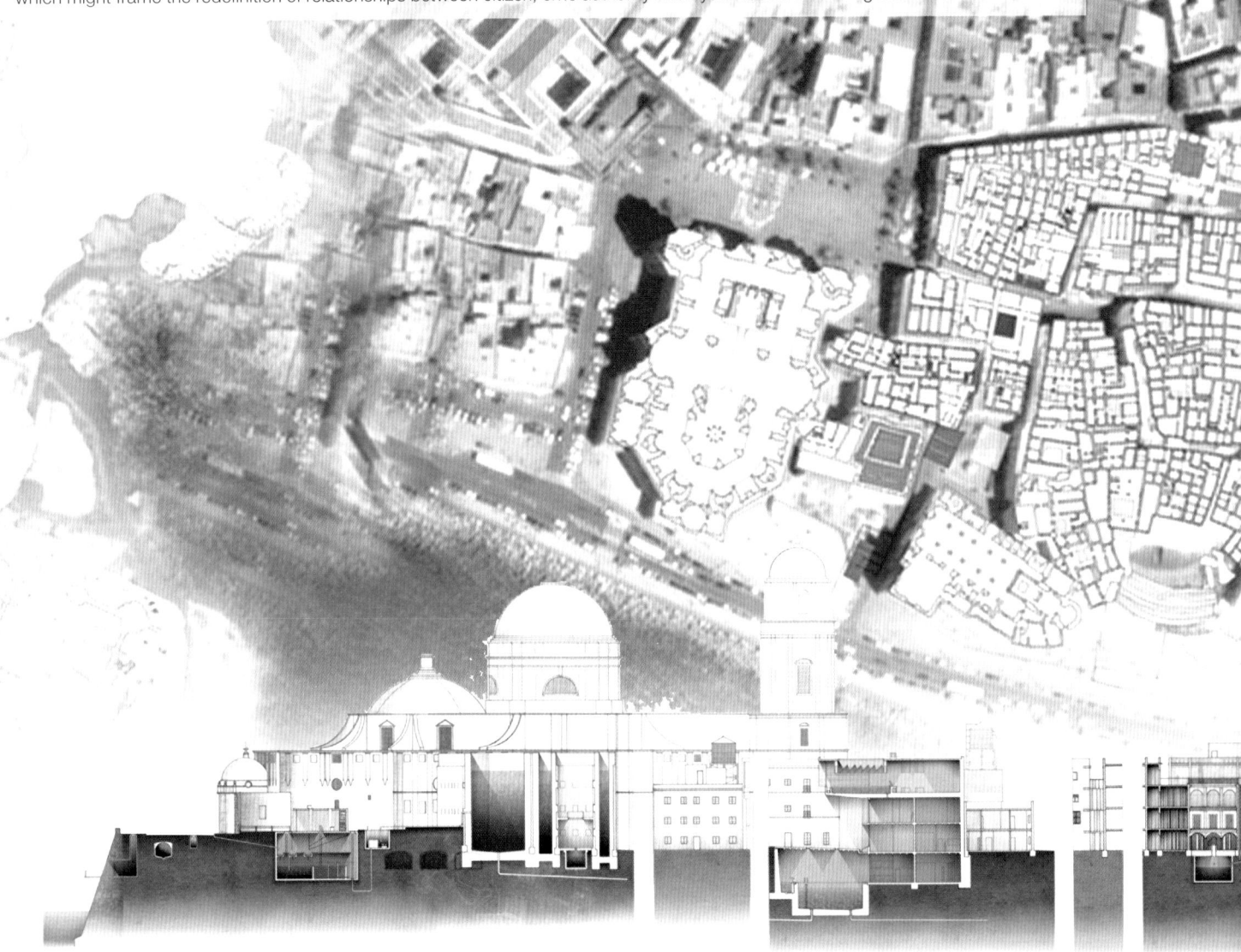

Rebecca Fotheringham *Hydroscape: the Hydropolitical Strand* 2008

The proposed *Hydropolitical Strand* is located in Cádiz's historic core, between the civic entrance from the Bay and the Cathedral on the Atlantic coast. This dense part of the city remains institutionally significant, yet suffers from some material and social decay. The *Cádiz Region Water Board* headquarters draws attention to the necessary accountability of civic water provision through its prominent location adjacent to the City Hall, arranged to allow accessible public archives and officials' meeting rooms visible from the street, and use of water in the environmental technology of the building. The *Hydrotherapy Centre*, embedded in labyrinthine residential streets, explores a more intimate, experiential engagement with water, and investigates structural and constructional implications of raised pools which might be appropriate in a city with little scope to build on open ground. The *Hydropolitical Strand* exposes the city's precarious relationship with the unruly and potentially threatening proximity of the saltwater Atlantic, offering architectural insertions which might frame the redefinition of relationships between citizen, civic authority and hydro-urban technologies.

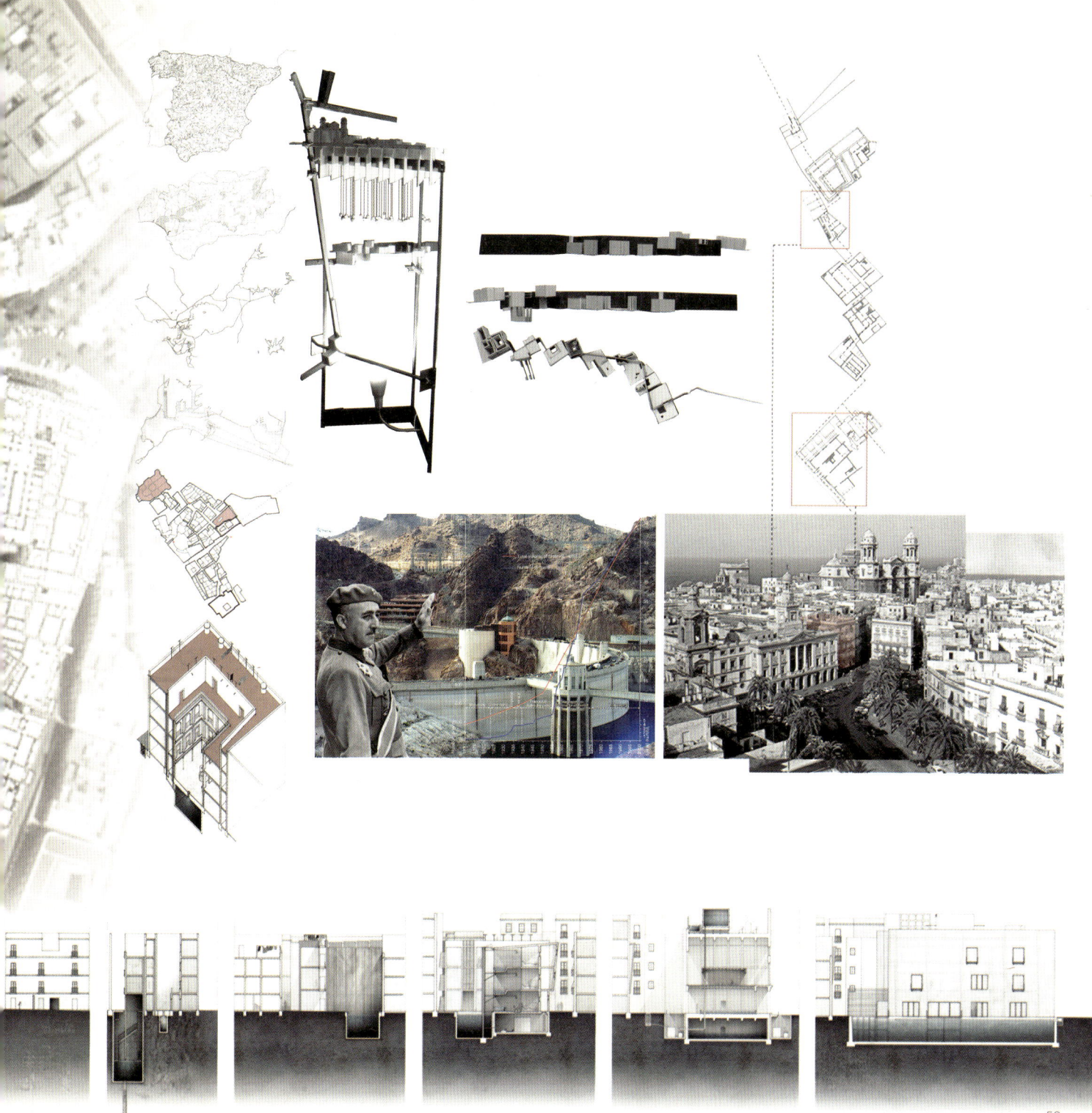

Adam Collier *Reprogramming the Ruptured City 2008*

Modelled and drawn investigations alongside historical research explored the metaphoric and pragmatic possibilities of one key site, the Puerta de Tierra, the eighteenth-century Land Gate at the neck of the connection between the Old Town and the New Town. Currently a traffic-dominated interchange, it is shown to have also been an area of geological disjunction. A programme was "uncovered" to include public routes of connection, exposure of Phoenician archaeology, and places of intense commercial activity which might "lock" new pieces of built city into a new urban geo-scape which has the potential for an enriched urban connection between two significant parts of the city. Geological metaphors have informed the architecture. Clusters of *Diapiric* towers house headquarters of the sherry industry and offer new commercial space to the city, alongside low-lying start-up facilities augmenting new public squares. A *Geophysical Laboratory* is located adjacent to the Puerta de Tierra, cantilevering over ground which exposes Phoenician tombs under excavation.

programmatic section through biocity commercial

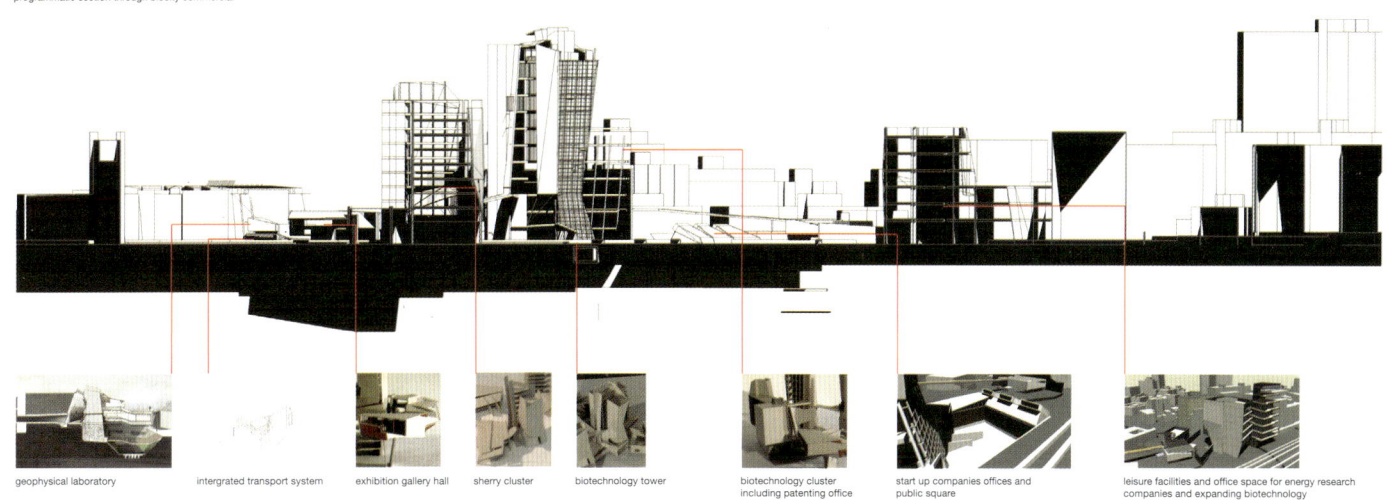

geophysical laboratory

intergrated transport system

exhibition gallery hall

sherry cluster

biotechnology tower

biotechnology cluster including patenting office

start up companies offices and public square

leisure facilities and office space for energy research companies and expanding biotechnology

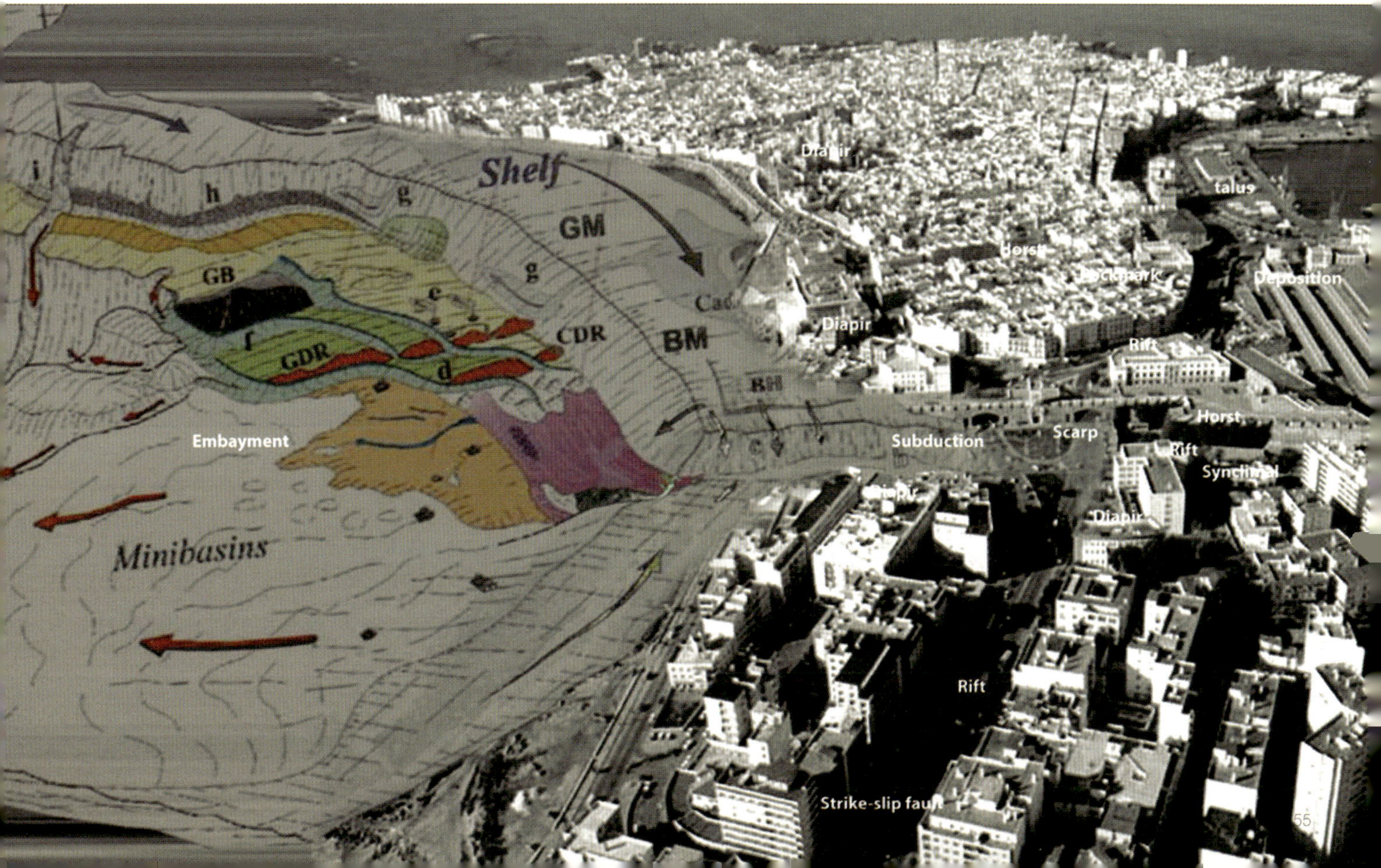

Sarah Castle *The Vesselled City* 2008

Fieldwork included the mapping of porosity in both the New Town and Old Town of Cádiz. The well sites, manholes and fortification drainage channels of the Old Town provoked a preoccupation with subterranean infrastructure, networks of flow and void familiar to historic European city mythologies. In the New Town, the porosity appeared to manifest itself most prominently through air conditioning ducts as the built fabric took on qualities of containment and flow. The tension between the city as sealed container (historic walls, military positioning) and as a medium to enable flow underpins the final series of proposals sited across the Cortadura, exploring this tension at the scale of *Habitable Vessels*. These include *Breach House, Fisherman's House, Social Housing* and a *Military Museum* occupying and re-connecting the remnants of the nineteenth-century Fort, currently bisected by the main road into Cádiz.

Michael Whitfield *Secreted Seams: Memories of Transgression* 2008

The project focuses on a relatively wealthy urban quarter in the dense Old Town where close morphological analysis has revealed looser, less well connected parts of the urban blocks, from casa patio to roof. This three-dimensional "secreted" field has become the ground for the project. Can an urban 'seam' of interconnected architectural proposals for programmes allowing migrants to "dwell" in the city (*Tailor's Bench, Street Seller's Lookout, Mosque, Gynaecological Clinic, Laundry, Advice Bureau*) be secreted into the private world of the city, perhaps even leaking into and enriching the public domain? Designing the urban becomes a question of who the design is for, and structuring the spatial arrangement of the city to allow for infiltration, appropriation and enrichment. The design proposals tactically extend to the interweaving of timber structures as an arcade threading its way through the least accessible semi-public parts of the urban fabric of the old city, only conceptually imagined as a whole.

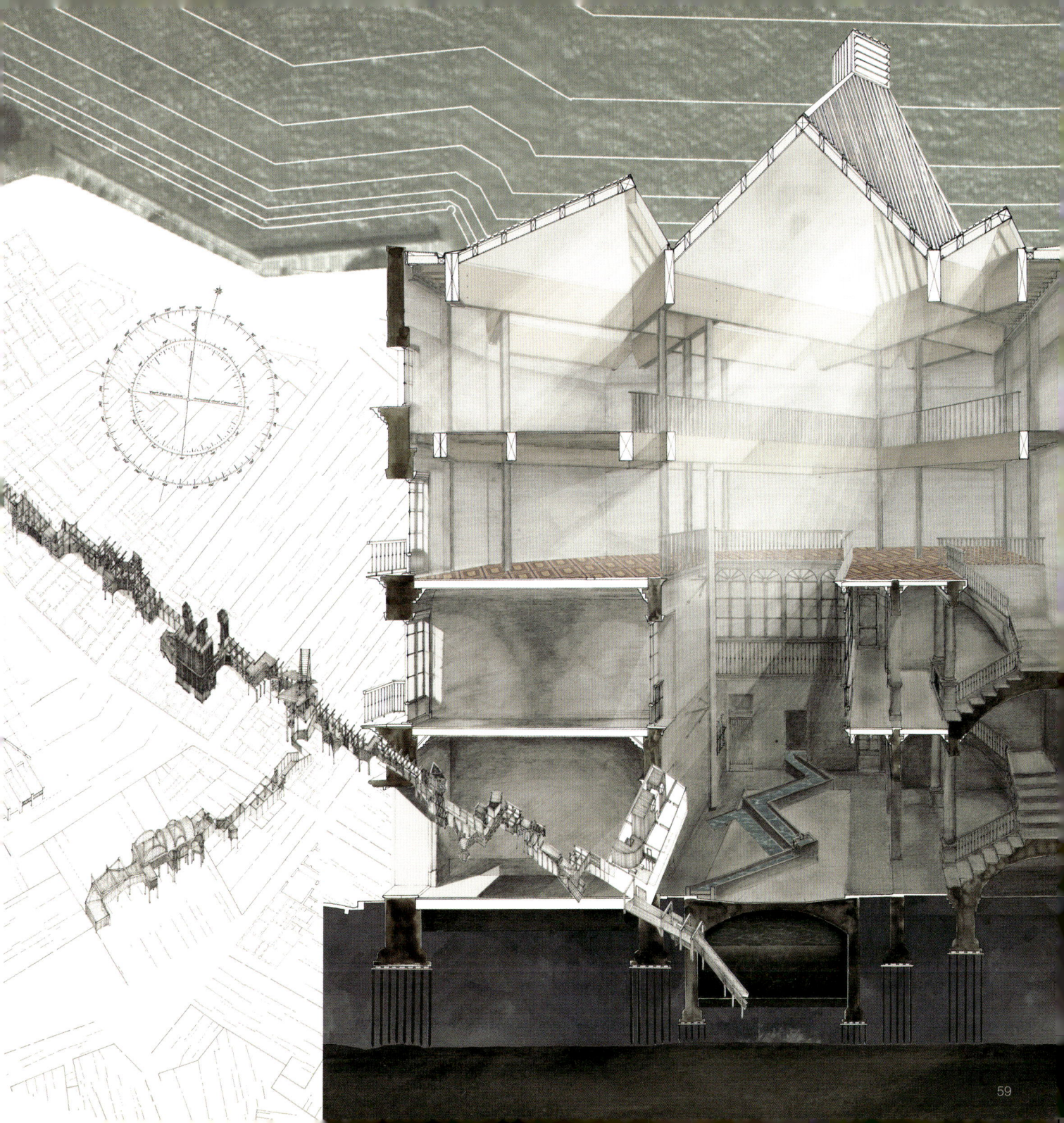

Jie Lin *City of Gaps: Threshold…Innerspace…Space Behind… Hidden Space…* 2008

The *House for a Lookout*, located in a gap adjacent to the recently revealed Roman ampitheatre, is revisited in the context of a final proposal for interconnected streets, programmes and events re-embedded in the existing urban fabric: market stalls, a cafeteria, a bath house, a launderette, and other service facilities for a transient population: an intricate three-dimensional urban section of a future Cádiz. The urban design begins to address the contested complexity of engaging with both strategic overviews and particularities of consequence on the ground.

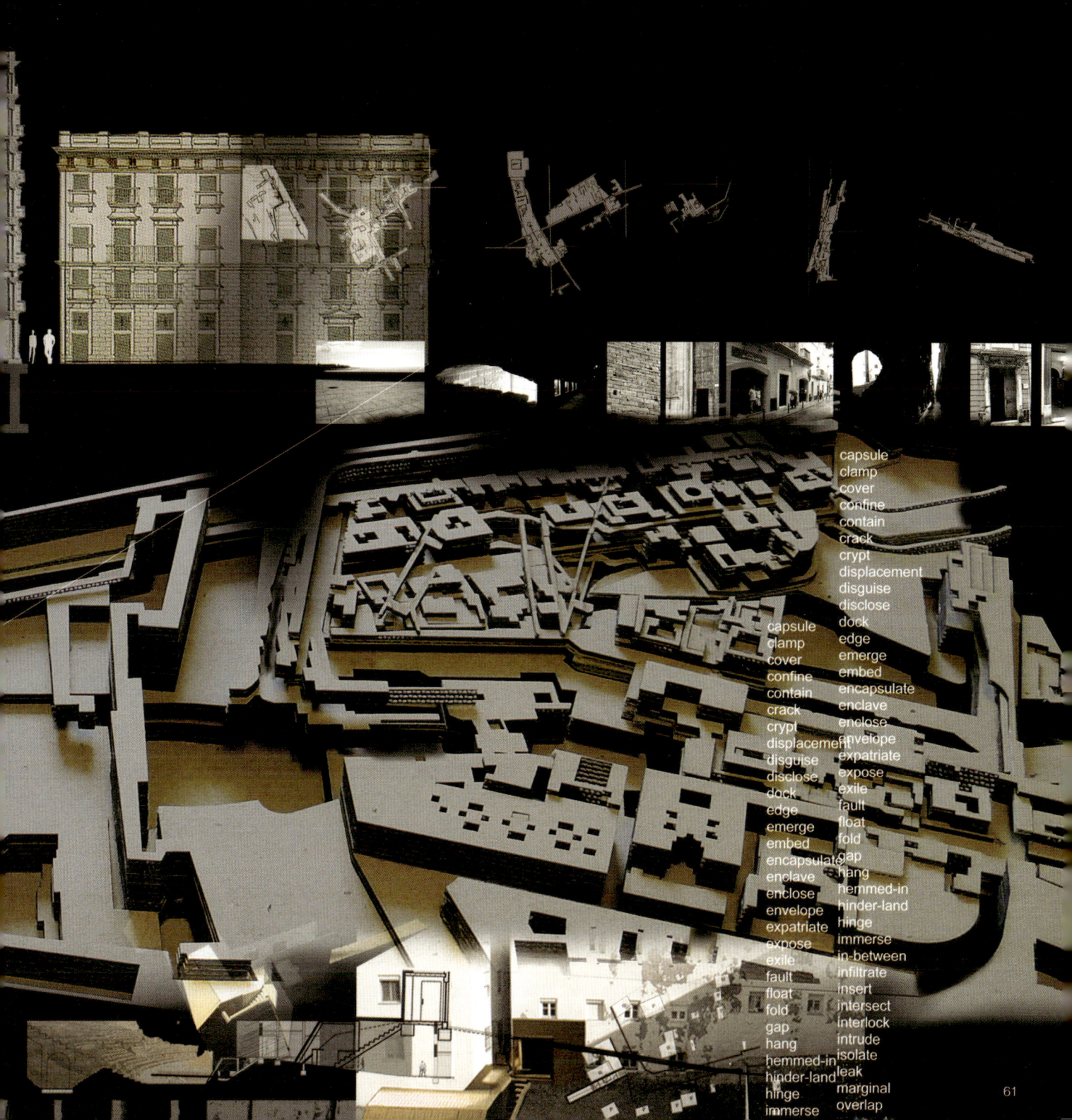

MAXIMVS

Ross Perkin *New Worlds within the Old Town* 2008

A new *Centre for Film in Andalucia* is positioned within a decaying urban area of the dense historic fabric of the Old Town. Early fieldwork, historical and technological research led to meticulous documentation of this part of the city, and the site became understood as a shifting ground latent with the material remains of a Roman circus. Ideas about porosity, typologies of entrances, the potency of the subterranean, excavation and the cultural role of spectacle have informed an urban strategy which literally and metaphorically reinforces the urban fabric. The architectural strategy is to precisely insert programmatic elements of *El Ciné de las Torres* which are held in mutual dependency while acting as support for the existing urban blocks. The new configuration of the cleared semi-public space is activated by film projection and public route. The material and spatial arrangement and language of the architectural proposal invents and develops a rich dialogue concerning weight, temporality and use.

CIRCVS

63

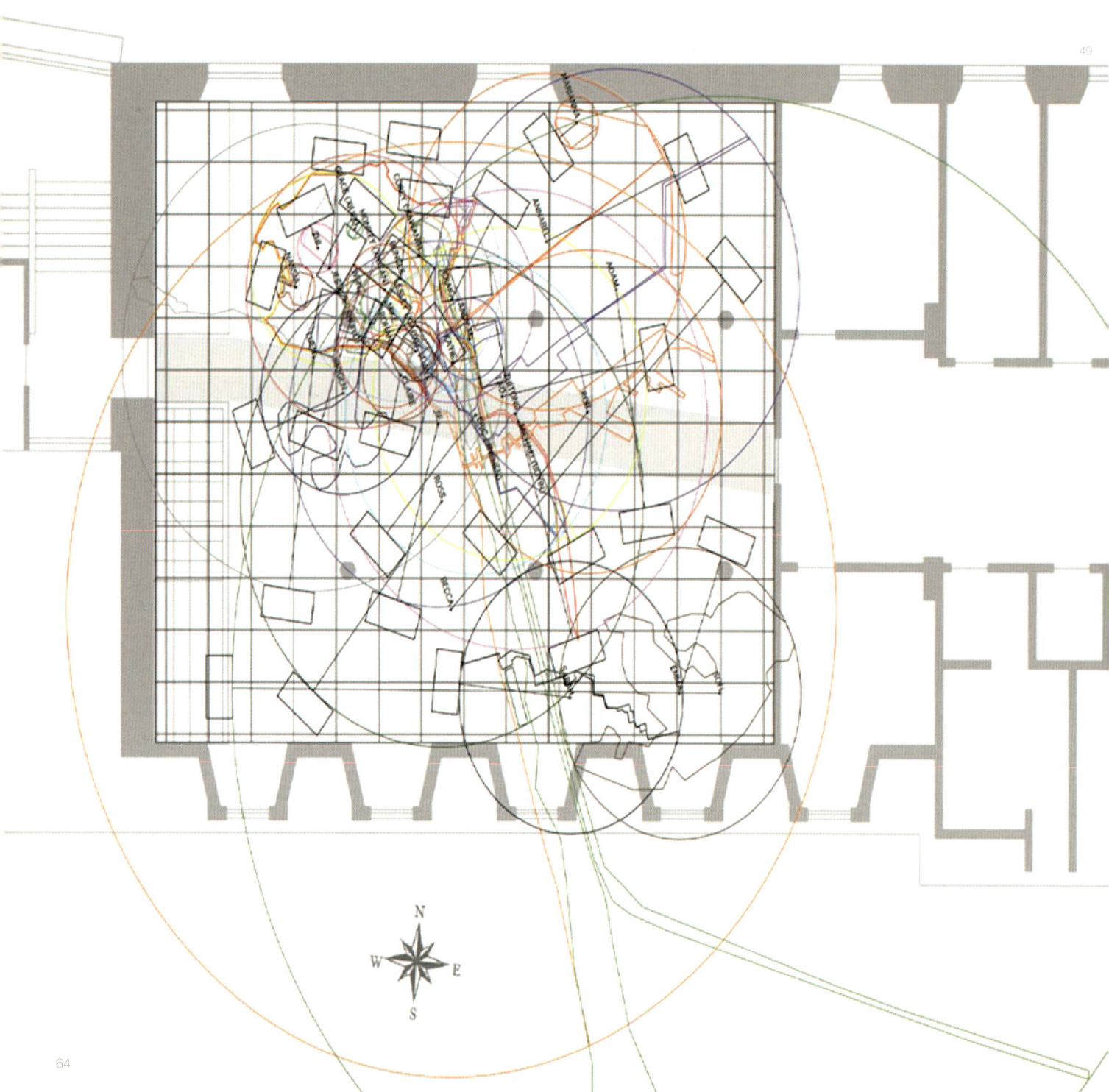

SaltCity: Cádiz Field+Work

49. Cádiz City Plan Choreography. Studio 5, Edimburgh, January 2007

Una selección de proyectos e investigación realizados en 2006-2008 como parte del programa de Máster de Arquitectura (MArch) de la Universidad de Edimburgo, dirigido por Suzanne Ewing y Victoria Clare Bernie. El trabajo presentado ofrece propuestas arquitectónicas, especulaciones y ficciones para la ciudad de Cádiz y sus tierras interiores. Al hacerlo, también suscita preguntas sobre la práctica(s) proyectual, las relaciones entre la investigación, el trabajo de campo y el proyecto, y señala la enseñanza de la proyectación arquitectónica como proceso que opera entre el ejercicio y el experimento. Esta publicación acompaña la exposición, *SaltCity: Cádiz Field+Work*, que tuvo lugar en la Matthew Architecture Gallery, 20 Chambers Street, Edimburgo del 4-29 agosto 2008. Se celebró un Simposio sobre los temas de la exposición el día 8 de agosto 2008.

"Conocemos las ciudades. Hemos explorado historias, desenterrado leyendas, traído a la luz posibilidades, probado ideas, analizado experimentos e imaginado futuros.

El programa MArch de dos años ofrece una oportunidad única para realizar un curso de investigación y proyectación intenso. Es la oportunidad de pasar tiempo mirando y leyendo una ciudad con el fin de realizar una proposición arquitectónica que sea más que simplemente un edificio - una nueva intervención dentro de una estructura urbana compleja, fuertemente cargada dentro del contexto social, político, económico, cultural e histórico.

Esta estrategia de trabajo de campo prolongado nos ha dado la oportunidad de ganar un conocimiento completo de la ciudad de Cádiz: las trazas de su historia, los temas complejos que la afectan hoy y los micro y macro organismos que conducen su futuro. A través de un programa coreografiado de trabajo individual y de grupo, y de investigaciones técnicas, teóricas, materiales y estructurales, se han examinado y probado tesis complejas, dentro de una variedad de escalas y medios.

El estudio ha propuesto veintitrés ficciones para la Bahía de Cádiz. Veintitrés futuros imaginados y profundamente arraigados en inquietudes teóricas y conceptuales individuales, cada uno de ellos apoyado en una exhaustiva investigación y documentación y cada uno de ellos identificando y respondiendo a una necesidad de la ciudad."

Emma Bush, Estudio de Cádiz

prefacio

La Universidad de Edimburgo ha ofrecido formación profesional en arquitectura desde mediados de 1960 cuando el arquitecto Sir Robert Matthew estableció la Escuela de Arquitectura. Desde entonces, la escuela ha crecido en tamaño y diversidad. Ofrece ahora una serie de títulos universitarios en Arquitectura, Historia Arquitectónica e Ingeniería Estructural con Arquitectura. Además, soporta un gran programa de Doctorado (por texto y/o diseño) y una serie de programas Máster en áreas tales como Proyectación Arquitectónica y Urbana, Medios Digitales, Diseño del Sonido, Diseño Sostenible y Gestión de Proyectos. La escuela también colabora activamente en la Universidad con una serie de otras especialidades, como Historia del Arte, Música, Estudios Cinematográficos e Ingeniería. Estas colaboraciones serán enriquecidas adicionalmente desde el año que viene con la fundación de una "Federación Académica" entre la Universidad de Edimburgo y la Escuela de Bellas Artes de Edimburgo (eca). Desde ese momento, la escuela combinará los programas de arquitectura de los alrededores y de arquitectura paisajista de eca con los programas del entorno construido de la Universidad Heriot-Watt para ofrecer un marco de educación arquitectónica que abarque las artes creativas y las ciencias del entorno construido. Es una iniciativa excitante que profundizará y diversificará las oportunidades de proyectación arquitectónica en Escocia.

La Escuela de Edimburgo ha desarrollado un carácter exclusivo en el que se combina el cosmopolitanismo, las prácticas ubicadas, los enfoques dirigidos por la investigación para la enseñanza y el aprendizaje y un espíritu de toma de riesgos intelectual y de consulta creativa. Este carácter emerge de un número de factores: la ubicación de la escuela en una universidad antigua y de investigación intensa, la creatividad y aptitudes de su personal académico, los excelentes estudiantes que atrae, y su posición en la extraordinaria ciudad de Edimburgo misma. Este carácter se ha puesto de relieve en el programa MArch y hallará una expresión particular en el trabajo que se verá en las siguientes páginas.

Stephen Cairns, Director de Arquitectura, Universidad de Edimburgo

El programa de Máster de Arquitectura de la Universidad de Edimburgo como existe hoy es el resultado de un proceso de transformación pedagógica y refinamiento que ha durado 20 años. El foco del año final del proyecto en la ciudad fue por primera vez establecido definitivamente a finales de 1980, y se estudiaron las implicaciones de ello para una secuencia de ciudades durante los 10 años siguientes. En el 2000, se introdujo la idea de un tema programático a nivel general que coordinaría el trabajo, primero para un proyecto basado en Ghent (*"Architecture as a Spatial Operator"*) y después de 9/11 Berlín (*"Architecture in the Age of Anxieties"*). Para esta etapa, el programa y el departamento de forma más general, estaba atrayendo atención internacional significativa por su planteamiento - véase, por ejemplo, la revisión publicada en la publicación japonesa *Architecture + Urbanism*, 413 (2000). Unos años más tarde, ciertos cambios estructurales que estaban teniendo lugar en la universidad dieron la oportunidad de reconfigurar el programa MArch a su distintivo formato actual de 2 años. El primero de los nuevos proyectos estuvo basado en Valletta (2004-2006) y fue dirigido por Adrian Hawker, y el segundo, acerca de Shanghai (2005-2007) estuvo dirigido por Dorian Wiszniewski. El proyecto de Cádiz - el tema de este volumen - es el tercero de la serie. El presente catálogo, que inaugura una nueva secuencia de publicaciones anuales basadas en el programa MArch, documenta con profusión de detalles el trabajo de los estudiantes y la pedagogía crítica y reflexiva de la líder del proyecto, Suzanne Ewing, ayudada por Victoria Clare Bernie que ha sido miembro consistente y clave del personal de MArch a través de sus diferentes transformaciones. Lo que considero que es crucial al programa MArch de

Edimburgo es el tipo de "apertura estructurada" que ofrece a sus estudiantes, proporcionándoles un marco poderoso de consulta sin presuponer respuestas específicas. Desde el principio, esto hace a la ciudad misma posar como una pregunta y al proyecto - con mucho entusiasmo - funcionar como esfuerzo colectivo de exploración e investigación en el que los estudiantes y los tutores son participantes activos, mientras que el período de 2 años permite que los proyectos emerjan en diálogo con un programa de material cultural, histórico y de investigación de extraordinaria profundidad e intensidad.

Mark Dorrian, Director del Programa MArch

introducción: campo

Este catálogo documenta la primera exposición de los proyectos del programa de Máster de Arquitectura (MArch) de la Universidad de Edimburgo, que ha sido explícitamente preparada para un amplio público. Es un registro de la práctica de investigación original que trata de proporcionar una visión general de la pedagogía y de los procesos característicos del taller de proyectos *Cádiz Field+Work* en 2006-2008. La estructura del programa MArch de la Universidad de Edimburgo trata de integrar la investigación y la proyectación en la producción de una propuesta arquitectónica para una ciudad europea específica. Fomenta activamente el compromiso con: el medio, la historia, la cultura, la geografía, la narrativa, la política, la tecnología y el arte. La Arquitectura que se produce en el programa viene descrita en varios medios: dibujos, pinturas, fotografías, bocetos, maquetas, películas, animaciones, textos descriptivos y analíticos, ensayos teóricos, instalaciones y representaciones. Describe un territorio intelectual e imaginativo, a la vez familiar y perturbador, a una disciplina cuyas tradiciones más recientes han tomado prestados, en vez de habitarlas, de los dispositivos visuales y de las investigaciones teóricas de otras disciplinas.

SaltCity: Cádiz Field+Work está estructurado alrededor de una cronología de dos años de estudio, señalando los aspectos clave de la estructura temática y resaltando las piezas significativas del diseño y la investigación. La narrativa comienza con **+Work (landschaft)**, una apertura de la noción de la eidética en relación con los proyectos arquitectónicos, trabajos de campo e investigación. **Hinge 1** describe un proyecto colectivo clave que plantea temas de temporalidad y multiplicidad en relación con lo urbano. **+Work (mēchanē)** refleja las relaciones entre el análisis, la interpretación y la irrigación, cuando las estrategias de la ciudad del grupo emigran hacia las estrategias espaciales individuales, las pruebas a escala ambientales y tecnológicas. **Hinge 2** consolida las proposiciones en una Maqueta de la Ciudad a 1:500, como un *locus* generador del proyecto integrador resultante, de la exposición y del informe, y el tema de la discusión final en **+Work (praxis)**. Se han seleccionado ocho interrogaciones individuales de proyecto para la exposición, que sirven para dilucidar los aspectos de la narrativa del taller.

La voz del del director del programa en el texto principal está entrelazado con otras voces - reflexiones de los estudiantes, de comentadores sobre Cádiz, de colaboradores en el taller y extractos provocativos del discurso arquitectónico reciente.

"Visité el estudio *SaltCity* en dos ocasiones durante el programa. Vi muchos esquemas inventivos e ideas ambiciosas, y la variedad me impresionó. Pero lo que más disfruté, y lo que se me quedó en la mente, fue la profunda contribución que esta pedagogía ofrece a la enseñanza del proyecto y a la arquitectura en su sentido más amplio. *SaltCity* demuestra una modalidad de aprendizaje que - de toda su visión vanguardista - nos vuelve a llevar a una cultura arquitectónica escalonada en tradiciones humanísticas.

Lo que más me impresionó del proyecto fue un credo de éticas sociales que lo penetraba todo. Hallé que este planteamiento ético era más interesante porque estaba totalmente enterrado en un modo de práctica de diseño. Por consiguiente, los proyectos no trataban de "hacer el bien" ni anotarse puntos. Por el contrario, su compromiso con la realidad deseaba hacer un mundo mejor.

La idea de hacer un mundo mejor, en lugar de otros modelos de corriente dominante de éxito - como ser un profesional sólido; proporcionar buen valor para el cliente; fiabilidad y eficacia comercial - es algo raro en la práctica de la arquitectura, pero es un paradigma poderoso para la orientación de la arquitectura como disciplina. Este programa, ha tenido un éxito especial en traer enfoques éticos para influir en los problemas urbanos típicos y a la vez contemporáneos, especialmente en los problemas del orden cívico que se tienen en cuenta para la interfaz entre las preocupaciones de la sostenibilidad y las necesidades de continuidad cultural de la sociedad. Aprovechando las historias locales y el carácter de situaciones particulares, el trabajo del estudio embebe sus propuestas en una realidad cimentada. Esta verdad al experimentar inyecta entonces típicamente un sentido de lugar en los esfuerzos para divisar un futuro positivo. Los diseños de algo nuevo se cimentan no solo en el contexto, sino también en el cuidado. Y este cuidado - un deber a hacer el mundo un lugar mejor - se convierte en un "deber de cuidado" ejercitado en el trabajo de imaginar.

No existe un fallo mayor y más endémico en un desarrollo urbano contemporáneo que el fallo de la imaginación. *SaltCity* demuestra una metodología de estudio en la que la invención y la perspicacia no solo florecen simplemente en un vocabulario de talento de otro modo vacío, sino en una fusión de estética y de ética. Este es el valor de tratar el estudio como lugar de investigación en el que la teoría y la práctica se unan entre sí en algún lugar entre la investigación de campo y los ejercicios en conceptualización. El logro de *SaltCity* es cimentar incluso la más frívola de sus viñetas en una estructura consolidada de comprensión, una que reinserte la historia humana en su sueño para reinvigorar una ciudad que ha perdido su floración."

Matthew Barac, PTEa (London),
Chairman, Architecture sans Frontières (UK)

field. n. el territorio que pertenece a una ciudad[1]

El programa del Máster de Arquitectura de la Universidad de Edimburgo dura dos años académicos de cuatro semestres y un verano. La estructura y el contenido del programa define el Taller de Proyectos Arquitectónicos como terreno de exploración y experimentación dentro de los confines potencialmente más didácticos del más amplio contexto educativo y profesional.[2] Toma como punto de partida la ciudad del estudio, el anclaje empírico, un lugar elegido por su potencial como territorio rico: una arquitectura, una ciudad, un clima, una política, una historia, una industria, un idioma y una cultura capaces de informar una comprensión de una condición urbana contemporánea (europea) Se llevó a cabo un viaje de estudios en el mes de noviembre del primer semestre. Los proyectos *Hinge* - tentativos colectivos del taller - tuvieron lugar en el mes de enero de los semestres 2 y 4. El trabajo del taller es un cambio de posición del taller de materiales, taller de diseño, laboratorio informático, biblioteca, archivo y campo. Los estudiantes trabajan independientemente y colectivamente en contextos dirigidos y autodirigidos.

La práctica del estudio estuvo guiada por las nociones de compromiso, negociación y narrativa establecidos por el científico y filósofo social francés Michel de Certeau en *The Practice of Everyday Life*.[3] Aquí se ve como las formas estratégicas, tácticas (e intermedias) de operar como individuos en una ciudad representan un potencial del proyecto arquitectónico crítico; para evocar la posibilidad de una comprensión generativa entre la investigación urbana (análisis) y la proyectación arquitectónica (proyección / especulación / habitación). La filosofía de la enseñanza del programa *Cádiz Field+Work* está respaldada por un compromiso a la colaboración, al diálogo y a la Arquitectura como praxis.[4]

El tema del taller del programa *Cádiz Field+Work* en 2006-2008 está basado en la necesidad y deseo de que la práctica de la proyectación arquitectónica esté conscientemente situada. Rem Koolhaas habla del futuro papel de la arquitectura como "la irrigación de los territorios con potencial" en lugar de "la disposición de objetos más o menos permanentes".[5] Esta declaración provoca un enfoque exploratorio a la comprensión: territorio (campo, terreno, emplazamiento); qué ´potencial´ puede tener (actitud programática); cuáles pueden constituir los actos de ´irrigación´(borrado, purgado, resistencia, fricción, intervención, aumentación, acrecentamiento). El reto del trabajo es principalmente uno de compromiso, de activación crítica del potencial imaginativo de la ciudad como: una idea, una historia cultural, una topografía particular y un despliegue de posibilidades tecnológicas.

El Programa de Máster de Arquitectura de la Universidad de Edimburgo en 2006-2008 ha colaborado con el Colegio de Arquitectos de Cádiz y con prestigiosos académicos y profesionales de Escocia, Inglaterra, América y España.

Cádiz es una ciudad atlántica en la costa suroeste de Europa. La Bahía de Cádiz - que comprende la ciudad en el istmo y cuatro ciudades más - se percibe actualmente como una zona metropolitana. Es una condición que plantea preguntas de la definición del campo urbano dentro de una topografía suelta de ciudad:tierra:topografía acuática. Históricamente, Cádiz ha sido un centro de comercio de sal fenicio, una ciudad romana, y una puerta clave de salida hacia las Américas. Hasta 1884 fue un meridiano náutico principal: un pivote cosmopolita significativo en las culturas del descubrimiento y la globalización; una *punta* de Europa, África y las Américas; un terreno de prueba para las tácticas militares y navales y un portal para los flujos de mercancías, gentes e ideas. Es una ciudad del sur, una península de la Península de España. No es una isla, es una forma de tierra separada y a la vez unida a la España peninsular, un territorio históricamente percibido como "otro" para Europa. Su situación atlántica la condiciona como lugar de cruda exposición - sal, viento y luz - y frágiles ecologías - peces, pantanos y plataformas costeras. La ciudad de Cádiz es el retoño decadente de un ambiente extremo. ¿Qué significa cultivar la vivienda y la vida pública en este contexto? ¿Cómo podría este terreno cosmopolita ser "irrigado con potencial" mediante reflexivo, y puede que radical, compromiso arquitectónico y urbano?

El tren AVE de alta velocidad conecta actualmente los 550 km de distancia de Madrid a Sevilla en 2 horas y media. Desde Sevilla a Cádiz en coche, tren o autobús se llega en 1 hora y media o 2. Cruzar desde la España Mediterránea a África se tarda 1 hora. Las personas del estudio viajamos desde Edimburgo a Málaga (2148km) en avión en tres horas y media, y a continuación a Cádiz (147 millas) en autobús en dos horas y media. Es una zona metropolitana relativamente desconectada por tierra, pero estratégicamente conectada por el mar. En un futuro probable donde la movilidad decadente actual - especialmente la del transporte aéreo barato y la infraestructura centralizada basada en tierra - no se pueda tomar a la ligera, ¿pueden las *SaltCity*, donde *sal*(t) se refiere al salario, a la producción material en los límites del tiempo y de la tierra, ofrecer pistas y descubrir el potencial para la generación de relaciones más significativas entre la vida de cada día, la producción y la espacialidad? Como la sal, que es un agente de deterioro lento (o rápido), que añade agudeza, extrayendo el gusto existente, ¿cómo puede la arquitectura ser un agente de resistencia táctica para ralentizar la

1   Oxford English Dictionary (Oxford University Press, Oxford, 2008)
2   Ewing, S "Between the strategic and the tactical: research driven projects and project driven researches in Cádiz/Edinburgh" paper presented at EAAE International Conference *The Urban Project* (TU Delft, 4-7 June 2008)
3   de Certeau, M *The Practice of Everyday Life* trans. Rendall, S (University of California Press, Berkeley, 1984)
4   Pérez-Gómez, A "Architecture and Ethics Beyond Globalization" ARCC/EAAE Montreal Conference on Architectural Research eds Fontein, L, Neukerman, H (Belgium, 2001) pp13-22
5   Koolhaas, R, OMA "Whatever Happened to Urbanism?" *SMLXL* (010 Publishers, Rotterdam, 1995)

ciudad, añadiendo sorpresa y placer, extrayendo poéticamente los atributos existentes y planteando nuevas posibilidades para la vivienda y la vida pública?

"…el sentido literal del campo como el plano horizontal sobre el cual el paisaje y los eventos estan acabados. Esto conecta el campo con el paisaje, la ecología y el urbanismo."[6]

+work (landschaft)

En el ensayo, "Eidetic Operations and New Landscapes",[7] el paisajista y teórico James Corner considera la relación entre el paisaje y la imagen, destacando la noción de "landschaft," donde el paisaje no se comprende ni como inocente - natural - ni como artificio - idea - sino como espacio vivido en el tiempo. Esboza una necesidad de los diseñadores de "equipar totalmente sus arsenales de operaciones eidéticas…"; sus recursos visuales: los dispositivos de mirar con atención, recuerdo, fabricación e imaginación que distinguen al hacedor crítico. Propone un foco de atención sobre "la lógica del hacer el paisaje en lugar de solo su aparienie".

"En el paisaje de pequeña escala y descontroladamente habitado que rodea incluso el pueblo más ordinario de Europa, han proliferado las industrias de servicio, estableciendo raíces, hallando un alojamiento de autoreferencia en un paisaje que ha perdido su coherencia. Parece apropiado examinar tales lugares para descubrir reglas posibles de intervención. Requiere de nosotros un tipo de cultivo, un tamizado para redescubrir un paisaje con propiedades críticas. Requiere de nosotros coser en el paisaje los inicios de una nueva arquitectura que tenga en consideración el espacio, la luz y la escala de material: los mecanismos específicos del lugar en relación con la cultura. En este paisaje estamos constantemente trazando conexiones entre la estrategia y el detalle con el fin de ajustar nuestras bases y nuestros puntos de vista del particular."[8]

El estudio comenzó con un simposio de investigación, seguido por un viaje de estudios de ocho días de duración a Cádiz. A la vuelta, los estudiantes llevaron a cabo un proyecto de diseño de tres semanas de duración de una *Casa de Observación* que estaría situada en relación con las fortificaciones de la ciudad. El simposio formuló una encuesta de temas y métodos con el fin de crear una base común discursiva. Se eligieron conscientemente las herramientas, guías y dispositivos del trabajo de campo ya que "el espacio de diseño"[9] había cambiado de posición de Edimburgo a un territorio menos conocido (por nosotros). La jornada entre la base y el campo y el tiempo transcurrido en el viaje de estudios tuvo en cuenta perderse, observar, recopilar, grabar, representar, poner en orden, leer, medir, actuar en la ciudad durante un tiempo, una primera versión de la comprensión a través del trabajo en el campo.

Los temas que estaban dirigidos a situar el estudio en un contexto español de postdemocracia política y cultural incluyeron: La Bahía como encrucijada biológica entre los flujos del Atlántico y el Mediterráneo; las lecturas geológicas del terreno que revelan fuerzas continuas de material de macro escala actuando sobre el tiempo; la ciudad islámica, la recuperación de la memoria (la Guerra Civil Española de 1936 hasta la muerte de Franco en 1975), el futuro del turismo, Cádiz como emplazamiento estratégico, historial militar y naval, la contaminación/desechos, el espectáculo, el trauma y la violencia en la cultura española. Se mostró el puerto como formando parte de una red Mediterránea/ Norteafricana muy particular (Cremer). La costa meridional de España se identificó como porosa, complicada por los flujos cada vez mayores de la inmigración (Perkin/Whitfield). El significativo trabajo de campo original incluyó el mapa de actividad del bullicioso antiguo mercado, un experimento en ritmanálisis[10] (Bush/ Brooks), la documentación de la porosidad del material - los conductos y las unidades de aire acondicionado - (Castle) y de la infraestructura del agua (Fotheringham). Un estudio de archivo posterior de la acción napoleónica en la zona, demostró la contención defensiva secuencial del núcleo urbano (Castle).

El control del acceso y salida al campo de la ciudad ha tomado históricamente una serie de formas con patrones relacionados de actividad. Una de las más visibles era la atalaya del siglo XVIII que ocupaba los tejados de las casas de los mercaderes, y que permitía que las vistas estuvieran orientadas hacia el puerto para vigilar las llegadas de los barcos/mercancías. Estas atalayas se entrelazaban con la estructura habitada habitual de la ciudad. Hasta cierto punto se convirtieron en espacios servidores, lugares de seguridad y retirada, a la vez con potencia óptica y conexión más amplia. Este *landschaft*, campo urbano comprendido como espacio vivido en el tiempo, se exploró a través de los proyectos de diseño de una atalaya contemporánea. Los proyectos requirieron una articulación de lo racional de la ocupación, la situación, la disposición y la lógica de consecuencia material. Emergen los idiomas de diseño - "idiolectos" inventados (una variedad de un idioma único de un individuo) - que dan permiso para pensar y moverse. Se convierten en una operación eidética de tipos, narrativas de un paisaje individual.

6   Allen, S "field conditions" *Assemblage* Issue 41 p8
7   Corner, J ed. *Recovering Landscape: Essays in Contemporary Landscape Theory* (New York, Princeton Architectural Press, 2000) Chapter 10 pp153-169
8   Macdonald, C, Salter, P "Bespoke Territory" in Middleton, R ed. *The Idea of the City* (MIT Press, Cambridge, MA 1996)
9   Wigley, M "Prosthetic Theory: The Disciplining of Architecture", *Assemblage* No.15 (Aug 1991) p20
10   Lefebvre, H "Rhythmanalysis of Mediterranean Cities" Kofman, E, Lebas, E eds *Henri Lefebvre: Writings on Cities* pp219-227

hinge 1

Cardea, diosa romana de - entre otras cosas - las bisagras de las puertas: "su poder sirve para abrir lo que está cerrado; para cerrar lo que está abierto."[11]

Durante el transcurso del estudio *Cádiz Field+Work* dos proyectos del grupo demostraron ser críticos para el desarrollo de las prácticas de trabajo y del contenido temático. El primer "hinge" (proyecto), *La Oficina de Plan(ificación) de la Ciudad de Cádiz [CCPO]* tuvo lugar entre las reclamaciones territoriales individuales iniciales del trabajo de campo y la investigación de escritorio del Semestre 1 y el trabajo de diseño estratégico de la ciudad y espacial del Semestre 2.

Este proyecto de 8 días fue una exploración de la "educación arquitectónica de ejecución". Participaron treinta y dos estudiantes (entre ellos ocho estudiantes del Máster de Diseño Arquitectónico Avanzado), trabajando con el Profesor Invitado de Arquitectura "Simpson" en 2006-2007, Ben Nicholson, y las tutoras del curso, Suzanne Ewing y Victoria Clare Bernie. Las instrucciones para la CCPO fueron trabajar juntos para recopilar y consolidar los 32 territorios y temas identificados hasta entonces por cada estudiante. *El Plan de la Ciudad de Cádiz fue presentado* a la 1 de la tarde del jueves día 18 de enero en Studio 5, 20 Chambers Street, Edimburgo a los Profesores Ben Nicholson y Andrew Benjamin. La *CCPO* estableció una matriz de relaciones donde se trazaron inicialmente los proyectos en un gráfico con el eje-x como elíseo-apocalíptica y el eje-y como autosuficiencia-dependencia.

"Este plan de la ciudad no confía en semejanzas o signos, no está expresado como una serie de territorios, ni tampoco como una colección de representaciones de edificios. Por el contrario, el plan existe a través de los enlaces que conectan esos edificios y territorios. Estas conexiones, que son normalmente invisibles al habitante de la ciudad, están resaltadas representativamente a través de un código secuencial de iluminación. La lectura es obligatoria. Es una representación teatral concisa de la urbanidad de Cádiz."

Sarah Castle

Las respuestas individuales de los estudiantes a la pregunta "¿Qué sigue pasando en la *CCPO*?" se realizaron poco después del proyecto, y un artículo del organizador del programa, sirvió para demostrar una rica gama de nuevas comprensiones de la potencialidad y de la naturaleza contingente de la práctica colectiva.[12] Al reconocer las condiciones de la temporalidad urbana y del fallo conectivo en la ciudad, el proyecto descubrió nuevas formas de imaginar y comprometerse con sus complejidades, procesos y lógicas para la acción.

Hinge 1 reconoce el movimiento hacia atrás/adelante/a través del proceso de diseño arquitectónico. Una posibilidad que distingue la relativa generosidad de un programa de estudio basado en dos años. El trabajo producido planteó preguntas sobre la práctica(s) de diseño individual y colectivo y sobre las relaciones entre la investigación, el trabajo de campo y el diseño. Se señala la enseñanza del diseño arquitectónico como proceso que opera entre el ejercicio y el experimento. Se expuso una imagen fotográfica agrandada de la instalación final, Película 1: *Haciendo la CCPO*, y Película 2: *Interpretando la CCPO*, en la Royal Scottish Academy Student Exhibition 2007.[13]

"Las medias son un enlace vectorial entre dónde estamos y dónde deseamos estar."

Robert Willis

"No tienen ni principio ni fin; ni puntos de culminación ni de terminación - pero siempre un momento central (*milieu*) y múltiples vías de entrada."

Euan Cockburn

"La pieza puede soportar muchos descosidos. Una multitud de largas y flacas piernas entrecruzadas, entrelazadas, un bosque de vides parasíticas, un museo de capullos silenciosos, maniquíes deformados, estalagmitas y estalactitas (estalagmedias). Cada una habla directamente del cuerpo y del movimiento (¿lento? ¿sofocante?) y abstractivamente del tiempo. En cuanto a la cuestión de escala, el uso de un material que es tan directamente humano lo une a su lectura, pero es igualmente de paisaje urbano y de organismo microscópico. Es todo esto y sin embargo es también la escala misma - la escala del proceso, de su fabricación, de su emplazamiento… Cada uno de los treinta y dos miembros de la clase pudo apuntar a la parte que es ellos…Es acerca del anonimato, acerca de interrogarse a sí mismo, interrogar sobre donde comienza, termina o se superpone una idea o se convierte simultáneamente en múltiples y una."

Emma Bush

"Cómo un grupo de personas se coreografían y se motivan a sí mismas es probablemente el reto más difícil en los proyectos de grupos grandes. La cuestión de quién es la persona que aparentemente está a cargo de decir a los demás qué hacer, qué ideas utilizar, qué ideas no utilizar y quién tiene que ir a comprar el café son problemas que se convierten en algo cada vez más insuperable cuanto más grande es el grupo…el ego personal fue una imposibilidad en el proyecto porque había tantas personas que tenían el derecho de propiedad por haber tocado las ideas en algún momento."

Andrew Brooks

11 *"numine clausa aperit, claudit aperta suo"*, Littlewood, R J A *Commentary on Ovid: Fasti Book VI* (Oxford University Press, Oxford, 2006) p40

12 Ewing, S "Experimenting with a performative project: The Cádiz City Plan(ning) Office" *Teaching and Experimenting with Architectural Design: Advances in Technology and Changes in Pedagogy* (ENHSA-EAAE Transactions in Architectural Education no 35, Thessaloniki, Greece, 2008)

13 Illustrated in RSA *Student Exhibition 2007 Catalogue* p.14. Exhibit no. 20 (Sculpture Court)

+Work (mēchanē)

"La palabra griega mēchanē ('máquina') se usa frecuentemente en contextos conectados con la irrigación…"[14]

En su introducción general a *The Practice of Everyday Life*, Michel de Certeau establece su proyecto urbano: "una investigación continua de las formas en que los usuarios… operan." Sus observaciones conciernen en primer lugar, con las formas de estar en la ciudad a través de las prácticas de los "lectores, las prácticas relacionadas con los espacios urbanos, las utilizaciones de los rituales habituales, el reuso y las funciones de la memoria a través de: las autoridades que hacen posible (o permiten) las prácticas de cada día…" y en segundo lugar, las formas de actuar en la ciudad mediante: "trayectorias", "tácticas" y "retórica", "leer", "hablar", "habitar", "cocinar".

Un desempaque tan cercano de la ciudad como terreno de operaciones sirve tanto al estudiante como al educador. Aplicado a la ciudad del estudio - un terreno relativamente o completamente desconocido - ofrece herramientas para la acción y pistas para la interpretación y al hacerlo, evita la prescripción: la ciudad de operaciones como una entidad viva, existente en el tiempo. El proyecto de una comprensión urbana es siempre, conscientemente contingente.

Todos los proyectos de diseño son hasta cierto punto versiones de la "línea de divagación" de Certeau: investigaciones escenificadas, aventuras no planeadas, descripciones pragmáticas, bocetos, borradores, pruebas, esquemas sorprendentes y ficciones ridículas. Para el estudiante, el programa y las instrucciones pueden identificar el campo sin prescribir un medio de operación mientras un discurso adicional del tutorial, la revisión, el proyecto colectivo y el individual pueden ayudar a trazar el camino. Hablamos mucho en el estudio acerca de trazar el camino de la práctica de diseño, para ser capaces de seguir el movimiento con el fin de proporcionar oportunidades de reentrar o de manipular la secuencia "fuera de".

La profesionalización del proyecto arquitectónico impulsa la práctica de diseño necesariamente hacia lo fundamentalmente estratégico, operando dentro del restrictivo orden del marco y fórmulación financieros, control de la ciudad, gobierno, legislación y gestión del riesgo. En este estudio, los estudiantes están expuestos a medios más tácticos de operación. Colocar el "hacer" de la arquitectura como parte de una comprensión más amplia del 'hacer' cultural de las ciudades es intencional y se dirige a provocar un compromiso crítico con los modos futuros de la práctica arquitectónica (profesional). Los estudiantes de proyectación arquitectónica son generalmente tácticos en sus compromisos iniciales con una ciudad de estudio, por lo tanto operan con "tacto": con precisión, con oportunidad y en relación directa con el instante, la circunstancia y la "improvisación", usando trucos y tenacidad.

Donald Schön ha argumentado que el taller de arquitectura ha pasado de la resolución del problema al planteamiento del problema.[15] La pregunta formulada al comienzo de la Tesis de Diseño de Cádiz fue ¿Qué necesita (desea) la Ciudad (el área metropolitana de Cádiz)?" Esta pregunta expuso el taller a la complejidad, ¿quién articula los futuros de la ciudad, y cuántos futuros posibles existen? Se posicionó la práctica de enseñanza del estudio:

- La ciudad (urbanismo)es un dominio rico pero discutido que requiere más escrutinio y análisis crítico.

- Se pueden descubrir y desarrollar nuevas y apropiadas posibilidades arquitectónicas mediante las estrategias usadas para "descubrir" o revelar la ciudad misma (ejecutable, diagnóstica, empírica, metafórica…)

- A pesar del debate actual sobre la desterritorialización de la arquitectura, podemos aprender y actuar de forma más precisa como arquitectos mediante el compromiso continuo con lo específico y lo particular, en lugar de con lo genérico o lo universal.

- El hacer crítico es un método productivo de análisis arquitectónico.

La "Tesis" se introdujo como término activo, una proposición relacionada con la ciudad que está explorada y desarrollada con el tiempo. Es una demostración de la posición personal descubierta mediante la investigación en el campo y en el estudio, prueba, propuesta de diseño y análisis reflexivo.

"La ciudad ha perdido el equilibrio necesario para mantenerse a sí misma."

Katie Nicolson

El tiempo y el ritmo del trabajo durante la Tesis de Proyecto fueron cuidadosamente coreografiados. Un proyecto de grupo de 2 semanas, Estrategia de la Ciudad, dirigido a establecer la multiplicidad de capas que constituyen la ciudad de Cádiz a través de la composición crítica y la archivación activa. El trabajo realizado incluyó: Un Refuerzo/mapa de Fallos, una Máquina de Bloqueo, Dispositivos de Fricción, una Máquina del Tiempo/Fortuna, Abrazadera/Bisagra/Herramientas de Izado, un mapa Pegajoso, una Guía para el miedo, Conductos de Dédalo (Laberinto Infraestructural), una máquina de lectura de Intervalos, un juego de Autosuficiencia. Emergieron paradojas a nivel general: una ciudad de tácticas materiales y desconexiones espaciales, una red metropolitana periurbana con fundamentalmente una tramapeatonal, una ciudad de ambientes refutados.

La estrategia espacial (acciones de campo) comprobaron las consecuencias de Estrategia de la Ciudad, tratando de resolver los problemas de emplazamiento, escala, producción y operación

14 Landels, JG "Engineering in the Ancient World" (Constable, London, 1998) p59
15 Schön, DA. *The design studio: an exploration of its traditions and potentials* (RIBA Publications for RIBA Building Industry Trust, London, 1985)

consolidándolos en una exposición colectiva con los estudios de trabajo transformados en un lugar de exposición. Si la ciudad está en un contexto que necesita o desea algún tipo de irrigación (física, cultural, política, social, económica), se pueden ver las mēchanē ("máquinas" singular?) en relación con el proceso de diseño: donde la mecánica eficaz (los arquitectos actuando en la ciudad) desarrolla las destrezas con el tiempo, adquiere el conocimiento de las piezas, y permite el funcionamiento suave, la sincronización, la temporización y la ejecución. La mēchanē potencial(como acciones irrigantes) incluyen la nominación, limitando/extendiendo, cercando/filtrando, el trazado material/desplazando, el control del umbral/la fluidez, la secuencia espacial/la repetición/el ritmo, la lógica de una parte con el todo.

Las Escalas de Consulta exploraron la operación de las proposiciones de proyecto a escalas 1:global, 1:1000, 1:100 y 1:local dirigidas a desarrollar las prácticas de trabajo que permitan la agilidad entre las escalas. Los movimientos de escala Urbana/ de la ciudad se probaron con los fragmentos creados a una escala más experimentalmente legible. Los fragmentos se probaron mediante mapas, planos y la construcción representada a una "distancia". La *Elaboración* fue una consulta detallada sobre lo que constituyen las respuestas tecnológicas detalladas a unas instrucciones, expresadas a través de la exploración de la construcción, del material, de la estructura, del entorno y de la respuesta sostenible. Los temas que emergieron pertinentes particularmente a Cádiz fueron: el microclima de la trama urbana - los flujos de aire y del agua, la masa térmica y de enfriamiento, la protección contra el viento y el mar; la fragilidad ecológica de la costa en lucha contra la contaminación histórica/ los contaminantes; los grados de energía/ autosuficiencia o dependencia del material; el paisaje/ las infraestructuras de producción y técnicas históricas asociadas - la irrigación, los sistemas hidráulicos y la extracción de la sal; el suministro y fabricación del material local-global; la política y el flujo de trabajadores emigrantes de la construcción en la región. Un período dedicado de investigación dirigido a informar de los proyectos de la Tesis en formas profundas e inesperadas. Al cierre, el trabajo de la Tesis fue articulado en una exposición instalada y documentada.

"…lo más interesante para nosotros fue la idea del laberinto subterráneo bajo la ciudad, creado por Dédalo, maestro artesano…Esta fue la forma en que concebimos nuestro modelo de una comprensión de Cádiz, deseábamos modelar una comprensión de los diferentes sistemas infraestructurales y de cómo encajarían entre sí en la ciudad. Esto produjo un sistema laberíntico cuando estaba inmerso dentro del modelo, pero cuando se miraba a él con más perspectiva, la lógica total era aparente."

Andrew Brooks, Sarah Castle

"5 de febrero.

Este fue el día en que lo empezamos. Asumimos los riesgos de los que habíamos estado hablando y pusimos cubos llenos de un líquido baboso en un trozo fino de tela clavada en un marco tambaleante suspendido por encima del suelo. Y funcionó. Habíamos añadido varias cuerdas, puntales y cables, pero como el marco se doblaba y distorsionaba en todo momento, se aflojó a pesar de haber estado muy tensado. Al unir el Nuevo Casco a Torregorda (ahora reestablecido), el Casco Antiguo se desplomó y torció, y el Puerto ganó mayor prominencia de soporte para contrarrestar esta acción. El vertido real era desesperado, y aunque el yeso chapaleaba y se vertía sobre los bordes, creando una forma de ciudad (¿sombra?) en el suelo, no hubo punto de ruptura absoluta (hubo un momento en que se tuvo que implementar con rapidez un soporte improvisado adicional) ¡pero lo consideramos todo un antifallo!"

Emma Bush, Sofi Tegsveden, Ross Perkin

hinge 2

hinge, n. un tipo de articulación que conecta dos objetos sólidos, que normalmente solo permite un ángulo limitado de rotación entre ellos[16]

Hinge 2, La Maqueta de la Ciudad de Cádiz [CCM], permitió el movimiento coreografiado entre las proposiciones proyectuales individuales en emplazamientos empíricos de Cádiz y la fabricación de un campo urbano reensamblado como el contexto para concluir los proyectos de la tesis en los últimos meses del programa.

Este proyecto de doce días tuvo lugar en el segundo año del programa trabajando con las tutoras del curso, Suzanne Ewing y Victoria Clare Bernie. Las instrucciones de la CCM fueron trabajar en cooperación para construir veintitrés proposiciones arquitectónicas continuas en sus emplazamientos y en relación entre sí a una escala 1:500, y utilizando una armadura urbana considerada y bien construida y un archivo de campo visual. *La Maqueta de la Ciudad de Cádiz* fue presentado a las 8 de la tarde del jueves día 22 de enero de 2008 (casi exactamente un año después de la presentación de la CCPO) en e estudio 4, 20 Chambers Street, Edimburgo, a una audiencia de estudiantes, tutores y visitantes invitados. Se hizo una presentación informal al Profesor Visitante de Arquitectura "Simpson" del 2008-2009, Iñaki Abalos.

"…se hacen veintitrés versiones de una ficción sólida. Como si veintitrés escritores trataran de escribir el mismo libro a la vez. Algunos de los caracteres puede que sean sencillos, si solo una persona está encargada de esa sección de la historia. Otros

16 Oxford English Dictionary (Oxford University Press, Oxford, 2008)

personajes podrían ser más complejos, colocando un sistema de colaboración, para escribir, sobrescribir y reescribir por encima…Colectivamente comprendemos exactamente que es lo que queremos decir con *nuestra* Cádiz Cuanto se extiende, dónde se difuminan sus fronteras hacia la nada, o donde acomete con precisión contra otras."

Emma Bush

Las respuestas individuales de los estudiantes a "¿Qué se hizo en *CCM*?", terminadas poco después del proyecto, demostraron que había surgido una confianza del aumento de la práctica colectiva comenzada en CCPO (*Hinge 1*), una autoría colectiva en el diálogo con una comprensión más profunda de las proposiciones individuales y el potencial de nuevas relaciones con otros proyectos. *Hinge 2* se puede comprender como una representación del movimiento hacia atrás/ adelante/ a través del proceso de diseño arquitectónico. Se "petrificó" el estudio *CCM* de 2006-2008 como consolidación de los movimientos territoriales colectivos. El ancla empírica se convirtió en mediadora, una manifestación del material en tarjeta gris, en acero negro, en hilo negro, en secuencia de película iluminada y proyectada. El potencial del territorio se había "realizado". La comprensión del campo de estudio perteneciente a la ciudad se demostró a través de la armadura posicionada en su relación con el territorio de arriba; la calibración de datos de las secciones de la tarjeta gris, el registro de la tarjeta gris de una morfología relevante urbana 1:500, y los actos acumulativos de irrigación de las propuestas individuales de diseño. Estas usaron el contexto de la maqueta como un nuevo anclaje, una interpretativa que engendró nuevas lecturas, especulaciones y posibilidades generativas.

"Una consistencia de material y técnica entre las maquetas individuales permiten un verdadero escrutinio a través de la ciudad; facilitado también por la propiedad común."

Andrew Brooks

"La Maqueta de la Ciudad de Cádiz funciona bien en el estudio, y realmente da una impresión de la forma/ topografía/ densidad…además de un sentido de llegada/ entrada a la ciudad desde la posición ventajosa elevada de las escaleras del estudio, acercando al visitante a *nuestro* mundo de Cádiz."

Andrew Mackie

"Las oportunidades surgen de las conversaciones, a menudo con el aspecto de argumento - las ideas se trabajan cuestionándolas, se desglosan y se vuelven a reunir…Por contraste, se llega a menudo al compromiso cuando la gente no cuestiona - es el momento en que alguien transige o el momento en que alguien aparentemente está de acuerdo, hecho algo mientras tanto y al reunirse otra vez hallar que ya

no "encajan" y tienen que acercarse entre sí de forma en que ambas partes estén menos incómodas. Esto es a menudo necesario para un proyecto de grupo, especialmente en un espacio limitado de tiempo para que ocurra. Existe un punto en que alguien necesita transigir o se necesita hacer algo."

Michael Whitfield

+work (praxis)

"Lo más importante es que la escuela tiene que enseñar al futuro arquitecto los elementos de la praxis: cómo hablar correctamente, cómo articular una posición…"[17]

¿Cómo obtiene un arquitecto el conocimiento de la ciudad y aprende cómo debe usarlo como base de la práctica crítica? La Escuela de Arquitectura puede proporcionar el marco temporal y pedagógico para desarrollar y hacer manifiestos los procesos de la práctica, preparando a los futuros arquitectos para más "zonas indeterminadas" donde el producto sea privilegiado. Hablar "correctamente" - con consideración, autoconciencia, tacto y seguridad - con las habilidades de texto, dibujo, maqueta, exposición, película y comunicación verbal. "Articular una posición" - tener una comprensión clara del conocimiento disciplinario relevante, conocimiento de las micro y macro fuerzas activas en el campo urbano, capacidad para identificar y analizar los límites y los constreñimientos, y saber cómo empezar a actuar como arquitecto.

Mediante el tema *Field+Work*, el estudio de Cádiz 2006-2008 ha cultivado la práctica de investigación original, desarrollado una filosofía pedagógica característica, y explorado las relaciones iterativas entre investigación y proyecto. El taller ha producido propuestas arquitectónicas ricas, sensibles y consideradas posicionadas en un campo urbano particular con el potencial de desarrollarse con el tiempo. Se puede ver *SaltCity* como una posibilidad de trayectoria de ciudades de economía lenta que reconoce los aspectos temporales del urbanismo, sugiere un escrutinio considerado y detallado y propone tácticas de compromiso con técnicas conceptuales y pragmáticas inventivas.

El compromiso con las resistencias particulares del campo de la zona metropolitana de Cádiz incluye el escrutinio de la trama espacial, disyunciones, tensiones. Se ha trabajado en cuatro territorios principales de Cádiz- el casco antiguo, el casco nuevo, el puerto y los territorios que atraviesan. Las inquietudes que han surgido en el estudio, varían en escala desde las redes infraestructurales a los momentos urbanos íntimos. Las propuestas culminantes se basan en la investigación personal, los resultados de las pruebas del proyecto individual de diseño y las estrategias ganadas de los esfuerzos colectivos durante 20 meses del estudio.

17 Pérez-Gómez, A "Architecture and Ethics Beyond Globalization" ARCC/EAAE Montreal Conference on Architectural Research eds Fontein, L, Neukerman, H (Belgium, 2001) pp13-22

En *Landscapes and Production: Cultivating a Biotechnological Field in the Bay of Cádiz*, **Emma Bush** explora la Arquitectura como un agente de calibración, irrigación e incubación en el muelle seco de la Dársena de Astilleros. **Rebecca Fotheringham** investiga el paisajismo de la gestión del agua en el Sur de España, y leyendo Cádiz como una Hidrópolis, ha basado sus propuestas en una serie de edificios entre la Catedral y el Ayuntamiento en el Casco Viejo, *Hydroscape: the Hydropolitical Strand.* Un nuevo distrito comercial justo fuera de Puerta de Tierra (la puerta del Casco Viejo) es la propuesta de **Adam Collier** en *Reprogramming the Ruptured City.* Su trabajo en esta área ha sido producto de la comprensión de una actividad geológica proyectada y de una inquietud particular con los lugares de ruptura que podrían catalizar las oportunidades de nueva habitación urbana, y que podrían proporcionar una lógica para la disposición arquitectónica y urbana. Desde la extensión del casco nuevo en el siglo XX, el límite de la ciudad se ha desviado y disuelto en playa/autopista/zona industrial. **Sarah Castle** en *The Vesselled City: Precipitating Human Activity at the City Edge*, ha estado trabajando con esta condición urbana contemporánea común y sobre cómo podría reanclarse a través del grano urbano y el uso residencial. La estadística descubierta en el flujo de inmigrantes junto a la narrativa que revela las necesidades y deseos incapaces de satisfacer explícitamente por la autoridad cívica ha motivado *Secreted Seams: Wanderings and Fabrics in Old Town Cádiz* por **Mike Whitfield**. ¿Se puede imaginar la arquitectura como una serie de momentos urbanos conectados que pueden engendrar encuentros transculturales en una vida pública enriquecida? **Jie Lin** en *Threshold...Innerspace... Space Behind...Hidden Space*, también explora el papel que la arquitectura, como intervención en la estructura urbana existente, podría jugar en aumentar la experiencia de la población transeúnte. Las propuestas de **Ross Perkin** en *El Cine de las Torres (New Worlds within the Old Town of Cádiz)* están literalmente basadas en los restos arqueológicos especulativos de un circo romano, y exploran cómo el cine, las películas y rutas definidas de público podrían reforzar conceptualmente, materialmente y experimentalmente una parte decadente de la ciudad.

Otros proyectos de la Tesis de Investigación y Desarrollo de la ciudad terminados el segundo año fueron:

David Ambrose: *Activating the City (Activación de la Ciudad): Protocols for a Sustainable Urban Coast* (Protocolos para una Costa Urbana Sostenible)

Andrew Brooks: *Mutable Spaces and Infrastructure (Espacios y Infraestructura Mutables)*

Emma Bush/Sarah Castle/Adam Collier *BioCity*

Eric Chen: *Hinging Seam (Costura de Bisagra)*

Euan Cockburn: *Mural Frontier (Frontera Mural)*

Wen Foo: *Rhythmic Assemblage, Heterotopic City (Asemblaje Rítmico, Ciudad Heterotópica)*

Claire Goodsell: *Resistance and Erosion of Urban Coast (Resistencia y Erosión de la Costa Urbana)*

Imogen Hogg: *Towards an Autotrophic City (Hacia una Ciudad Autotrópica)*

Craig Hutchinson: *Re-entering the City: (Reentrando en la Ciudad): Cádiz in Friction (Cádiz en Fricción)*

Jessica Ji: *Dilating Edge (Borde Dilatante)*

Andrew Mackie: *(Sea) Gate (Puerta del Mar)*

Kate Nicholson: *Microsurgery, Ossiointegration and the Taphonomic Boundary (Microcirugía, Osiointegración y el Límite Taponómico)*

Cory Wang: *Host/Guest (Anfitrión/Invitado)*

Tao Wang: *Drifting Field (Campo de Desviación)*

Robert Willis: *City of Friction (Ciudad de Fricción)*

Tong Wu: *Augmented Boundaries (Límites Aumentados)*

Boyin Yang: *Shifting Boundaries in the Mechanism City (Desviar los Límites en el Mecanismo de la Ciudad)*

La producción arquitectónica en el estudio *Cádiz Field+Work* 2006-2008 se ha caracterizado por una apertura a la exploración colaboradora, en un rigor de operación, de documentación, de hacer y rehacer. El trabajo del taller probablemente se ha acercado lo más posible al compromiso con la complejidad refutada del proyecto urbano al operar en las márgenes de la arena académica convencional: cuando "fuera de lugar" durante un viaje de estudios y trabajo de campo o al operar colectivamente, experimentar en el Primer año con un proyecto para construir un Plan de la Ciudad, y en el Segundo año, al construir una propuesta de Maqueta de la Ciudad. Cada instante señala las deficiencias de los proyectos de una sola visión o de la Arquitectura como únicamente producto u objeto. La coexistencia y proximidades de lo estratégico (perspectiva general, operaciones colectivas en la ciudad) con lo táctico (excursiones y diversiones individuales) permite la receptividad necesaria para cambiar las estrategias y tácticas de investigación que pueden profundizar el potencial transformativo de ambos, Trabajo y Campo en la Arquitectura.

acknowledgements

Cádiz Studio 2006-2008:
Programme Leader: Suzanne Ewing
Studio Tutor: Victoria Clare Bernie
Academic staff: Stephen Cairns, Fiona Maclachlan,
Remo Pedreschi
Specialist tutors: Keith Ballantyne, Dominic Echlin,
Cristina Gonzalez-Longo, David Narro, Andrew Stoane,
Dimitris Theodossopoulos, James Wild

Master of Architecture (Design) students:
David Ambrose, Andrew Brooks, Emma Bush, Sarah Castle,
Jinchen Chen, Euan Cockburn, Adam Collier, Wen Foo,
Rebecca Fotheringham, Claire Goodsell, Imogen Hogg,
Craig Hutchinson, Jie Lin, Andrew Mackie, Kate Nicholson,
Ross Perkin, Sofi Tegsveden, Mike Whitfield, Rob Willis

Master of Architecture (Studies) students:
Jessica Ji, Tao Wang, Jia Wang, Zhitong Wu, Boyin Yang

Msc in Advanced Architectural Design students (2006-2007):
Annabel Cremer, Rohan Goregaonkar, Xiaoyan Hou,
Marianna Kotilea, Xiaoxi Song, Nassia Spyridaki, Grace Tao,
Sofi Tegsveden, Cheng Zhi

Visitors/critics:
George Simpson Visiting Professor 2006-2007
Ben Nicholson (Art Institute of Chicago)
George Simpson Visiting Professor 2007-2008
Iñaki Abalos (ETSAM, Abalos & Herreros Architects, Madrid)
Matthew Barac, Andrew Benjamin, Ella Chmielewska,
Mark Dorrian, Colin Fraser Wishart, Soledad Garcia Ferrari,
Adrian Hawker, Dean Hawkes, David Higdon, David Jamieson,
Ray Lucas, Alona Martinez, Jane Paterson, Chris Smith,
Harry Smith, Sarah Wigglesworth

Fieldtrip support:
Colegio Oficial de Arquitectos de Cádiz
Ramón Pico Valimaña, Arquitecto, Decano
Tomás Carranza Macias, Arquitecto,
Jefe del Área de Actividades
Juan Miguel Canca, Arquitecto, Cádiz
Archivo Historico Municipal de Cádiz

Administration + support:
Course secretary: Leigh-Anne Pieterse, Carolyn Wilkinson
Admissions, field trip: Catherine Carmichael, Lindsay Hunter
Workshop/studio installation: Alistair Craig, Allan Ramsay
IT support: Ian Gunn, Geoff Lee
Media support: Rachel Travers, John McGovern
Research support: Ross Laing, Anne-Sofie Laegran

Exhibition/publication:
Author + curator: Suzanne Ewing
Associate curator: Victoria Clare Bernie
Exhibition Awards: Emma Bush, Sarah Castle, Adam Collier,
Rebecca Fotheringham, Jie Lin, Ross Perkin, Mike Whitfield
Translation to Spanish: Integrated Language Services,
School of Management and Languages, Heriot-Watt University;
Cristina Gonzalez-Longo
Proof reading: Eddie Clark

Support and funding from the School of Arts, Culture and
Environment, University of Edinburgh as a pilot project
demonstrating research-teaching linkages.
Additional funding is acknowledged from:
University of Edinburgh Development Trust, Small Project Grant
University of Edinburgh Knowledge Transfer Fund

With advice and encouragement from:
University of Edinburgh Festivals Office: Lorna Brain

Photo credits:
All photos and images used in this publication have been
produced as part of the 2006-2008 Cádiz Studio unless
otherwise indicated. All photos and images are protected by
copyright and may not be reproduced without permission.
Every attempt has been made to seek copyright permission
where appropriate. No part of this publication may be
reproduced without the written permission of the author.

Graphic design: Julie Robinson, Graphics Lab,
Learning Technology Section, University of Edinburgh

Printed by: J Thomson Colour Printers Ltd, Glasgow

ISBN: 978-0-9559706-0-3

FSC

Mixed Sources
Product group from well-managed
forests, controlled sources and
recycled wood or fiber
www.fsc.org Cert no. TT-COC-002242
© 1996 Forest Stewardship Council

75%